Discovering Biblical Treasures

Understanding 1 Timothy

Using Semitic Bible Study Methods with a new foundation

Michael Harvey Koplitz

Sandra Jean Koplitz

Table of Contents

Introduction

When a person is baptized as an infant and grows up in the church, their religious DNA assimilates different paradigms. The church has a message to give about Jesus Christ and His importance. Very few people study the theology and doctrines of the church to determine for themselves the accuracy of the church. The Proto-Orthodox church, which survived the pressures of the Roman Empire, decided to oppose any expression of Christianity that did not fit its dogma in its infancy. In addition, the Proto-Orthodox church would permanently destroy any writings that the rival Christians had developed.

The Gnostic Christians of Northern Egypt viewed the life of Jesus of Nazareth in a completely different way than the Proto-Orthodox church did. They saw the message about the Kingdom of Heaven as the vital purpose of Jesus. His birth, death, and resurrection are not mentioned in the Gnostic Gospels. However, did the Proto-Orthodox church destroy the Gnostic Gospels when they crushed said movement? The answer is yes and no. Yes, they destroyed what they got their hands on. No, because in 1948, copies of the Gnostic religious books were discovered in Alexandria, Egypt. Once these documents were translated, the world learned what the Gnostic Christians believed. It is fascinatingly different than what the Proto-Orthodox said about these followers of Christ.

Why is this understanding critical? Much research points to a different situation in the early years than what the church espouses. A lot of this information is available to anyone today. However, the Seminaries and churches will not openly discuss these other writings about Jesus and His disciples. The scholars teaching in most Seminaries have learned their lessons from the church and closed-minded mentors who refuse to look at other possibilities. This is because the Western European world took Christianity and changed it from a Near Eastern religion to Western religion.

There is a theory that Paul converted Mithras House Churches into Jesus House Churches. This is clear from the connection between the Mithras' and Christianity's rituals. For example, baptism was the initiation ritual of Mithras. Communion did not originate with Jesus. This ritual was a part of Mithras, where the followers would share his flesh (bread) and drink his blood (wine). There are many more rituals that Christianity picked up from Mithras. A good reference is "Christianity's Need for Mithras," which the author wrote.

Did Paul create the churches in the letters he sent, which comprise the New Testament, and if so, they must have been Jewish groups who became Jewish Christians? They would have continued with their Hebraic rituals and saw Jesus of Nazareth as the Messiah that the prophets of old had promised. They would have adopted many of Jesus' teachings and tried to live by them. The letters in the New Testament are written in Greek. However, most Jews in the Roman Empire did not speak Greek; instead, they spoke Aramaic and Hebrew. These congregations would not have understood a Greek letter from Paul.

Therefore, the letters in the New Testament must have been written in Aramaic and then transliterated into Greek. The same can be said for the Gospels, all of them. The church, over the centuries, decided who wrote the Gospels and their intent. The only Gospel we can assign to a writer is Luke. The other three are up in the air about who wrote them. While in Seminary, the author was taught that the entire New Testament was originally written in Koine Greek. However, that raised the question, "Did Jesus speak Greek?" The Seminary instructors said, "no, Jesus did not speak Greek." Then the New Testament, especially the Gospels, must have been written in Aramaic. After all, Jesus spoke Aramaic and Hebrew.

We know this because He was a poor *tekton* (a stonemason or carpenter) from an impoverished city named Nazareth. Being born to a Jewish family in Galilee, he would have learned the traditions of His people and trade. He would have learned to speak Aramaic, the language of the area. He would have learned Hebrew because that was the language of the synagogue and the Temple in Jerusalem. In other words, Hebrew was the language of God, and Jewish males learned the language.

Suppose you are ready to toss this manuscript into the nearest trash can or delete it off your electronic device at this point in the introduction. In that case, the writer has your attention. This is the reaction when the writer has spoken with persons who had been indoctrinated into the church's position since birth. The author did not come into the church environment until he was 35. Therefore, the church's paradigms, dogma, and doctrine were not a part of his DNA. Instead, he questioned a lot. He found many inconsistencies between the Bible and the doctrines of the church. Seminary was an experience to learn what the church had evolved into two-thousand years after the death of Jesus.

There are more parts to the premise that the New Testament was originally written in Aramaic and will be explored. For the reader to grasp the subsequent phases of the proof, an open mind is critical.

Culture and Language

Let us continue in the journey of examining the New Testament to determine its original language. Nothing in stone tells us that Aramaic is the Original Language of the New Testament. However, nothing says that Koine Greek was the original language of the New Testament either. Therefore, we have two theories about the original language of the New Testament. The author admits that the Seminary he attended drove home the belief that the Old Testament was written in Hebrew, except for a few spots. The New Testament was initially written in Koine Greek.

The writers' research has been searching for the original meaning of Scripture for many years. The methodology for this work is called "Ancient Bible Study Methods." The method was developed by Dr. Anne Davis of the Bible Learning University in Albuquerque, New Mexico. The author studied this method with Dr. Davis as his mentor. It became clear that the search for the original meaning of the Scriptures requires that the culture and language be examined. So, the author's methodology is Dr. Davis' work, plus his Ph.D. studies combining the method, culture, and language.

The language examination is easy for the Old Testament because it was written in Hebrew, and about one-half of Daniel is in Aramaic. It does not take long to realize that idioms and figures of speech in the Hebrew of the Old Testament revealed a lot about the people and situation of the day when the scrolls were written. The Targums were a valuable resource because they are the Aramaic translations the rabbis did for the people living outside of Judea. The rabbis added commentary to the Targums because they knew that some of the idioms and speech used in the Near East would not translate well into the different areas where the Jews lived.

The culture of the Near East has been essentially the same in many aspects since the days of Jesus. Many practices of Jesus' day are still in use today. The culture of the Jews of the Near East is built into the language. Often an Aramaic or Hebrew word has a deep meaning that is only fully understood by natives living in that culture. The Old Testament is filled with cultural items that do not need to be spelled out because the people knew their culture in the author's time.

Suppose the New Testament in Koine Greek is a transliteration of the Aramaic. The culture, figures of speech, and idioms will be easily identified when examining the Peshitta (the Aramaic version of the New Testament). Indeed many of the so-called difficult words of Jesus are not tricky when examined in the light of the culture of Jesus' day. An example is "faith to move a mountain," Jesus said these words to His disciples. The church determined that this meant complete faith in Jesus. From the western European Greek point of view, that makes sense. What else could it possibly mean?

"Faith to move a mountain" is an Aramaic idiomatic expression. What Jesus said to His followers when he said this is that his disciples needed to be faithful so that they could change the "government's view through their words." The governing body for Judaism resided on the top of a mountain. Jerusalem, with its Temple, was built on the top of Mount Zion, a very tall mountain. This idiom survived because the Aramaic Gospels were transliterated into Koine Greek. Numerous other examples support this position.

Suppose the culture and language idioms of Jesus' day can be found in the Koine Greek because it was transliterated. In that case, it supports the theory of the Aramaic versions being the original language of the Gospels and possibly even more.

The Aramaic Version of the New Testament

The Peshitta is the accepted Aramaic translation of the New Testament for many churches of the East. Peshitta means "simple, true, direct, and original." It is a collection of scrolls that were compiled in 150 CE. There were some revisions to the Peshitta in the fifth and sixth centuries. The Greek version of the New Testament is a transliteration of the Peshitta.[1]

For centuries, the Catholic church has used the Latin version of the Bible, the Vulgate, and still uses it. The Vulgate was developed around 350 CE by Jerome by order of the Pope at that time. Erasmus (1466 – 1536) was the person who put together the Greek New Testament for the Catholic church.

"The New Testament, brought to light in the original Greek tongue, was compiled and made available for humanity to study and learn. Although working under and deeply associated with the Roman Catholic Church, the learned scholar declared his disagreement with those who wanted to keep the Scriptures from the common people. He said, "If only the farmer would sing something from them at his plow, the weaver moves his shuttle to their tune, the traveler lighten the boredom of his journey with Scriptural stories!" Little did he know that the work he was about to produce would change the world forever. This Greek New Testament, in printed form, would become the standard of the New Testament, launching the translations of Martin Luther and William Tyndale into the world. Thus, fulfilling his dream that all men would read the

---

[1] Rocco A. Errico and George M. Lamsa, *Aramaic Light on Galatians through Hebrews: A Commentary Based on Aramaic, the Language of Jesus, and Ancient near Eastern Customs* (Smyrna, GA: Noohra Foundation, 2005).

Bible for themselves in their common language. His new "study Bible" had two main parts, the Greek text, and a revised Latin edition, which was more elegant and accurate than the traditional translation of Jerome's Latin Vulgate. Erasmus prefaced this monumental work of scholarship with an exhortation to Bible study. He proclaimed that the New Testament contains the "philosophy of Christ," simple and accessible teaching with the power to transform lives."[2]

The church recognized Erasmus' Greek New Testament in 1515 CE. The church in the Near East has been using the Peshitta as the original language of the New Testament since 150 CE. If the Greek New Testament was important to the church as an original language, then why did it adopt the Vulgate in 350 CE? The church should have adopted the Greek New Testament at the beginning.

The Peshitta, translated into English, is used to examine Paul's letters. The rest of the methodology that the author developed for Ancient Bible Study Methods is the framework of this research.

---

[2] "Erasmus Greek New Testament," Insight of the King, accessed February 18, 2022, https://www.insightoftheking.com/erasmus-greek-new-testament.html.

The Messianic Tradition Change

One problem for Peter and the Disciples was that they claimed Yeshua to be the Messiah that the prophets of the Hebrew Scriptures spoke. However, Yeshua did not do what these traditions said. The main tradition was that the Messiah would destroy oppressive Romans and reinstate the Kingdom of Israel. Yeshua would then be declared the king and sit on David's throne in Jerusalem. That did not occur.

None of the messianic traditions of the day worked. So, what was the new movement going to do? They turned to the prophets and discovered Isaiah 50-53. These chapters are referred to as the Suffering Servant chapters. The Yeshua movement decided that the Suffering Servant was Yeshua. The portrayal of Yeshua's life does fit the Suffering Servant chapters. However, rabbinical interpretation then and now sees the Suffering Servant as the nation of Israel. Indeed, these chapters do describe the history of Israel. Nations have wanted to destroy the Jewish people since the time of Abraham.

The diaspora from the Babylonia Exile and the Assyrian invasions looked to squelch the Jewish people. The LORD promised that a remnant of the people would always survive. That is true throughout the 4,000-year history of the Jewish people. Many nations tried to destroy them, and the LORD intervened to ensure that a remnant of the people survived.

Paul must have been convinced in his encounter with Yeshua on the Damascus road that Yeshua was the Suffering Servant. It is clear from Paul's writings that he did believe this. For Paul, the Messiah was the Spiritual Messiah that the Kabbalah spoke. The

Kabbalah says that there will be two Messiahs. This theology is based on Zachariah 9:9. The first Messiah is Messiah ben Joseph. This Messiah was to restore the Kingdom of Heaven, a spiritual Kingdom. The second Messiah will be Messiah ben David. This Messiah was to restore the Kingdom of Israel. The Midrash from the Kabbalah did not state that the Messiah was two different souls.

The Kabbalah

There is a large amount of material in print about the Kabbalah. The Kabbalah referred to is Moses's Secret Work from Mount Sinai. Legends say Moses received three items on Mount Sinai when he met the LORD. The first is the written law. The written law is called the Torah. The second is the oral law. The oral law was put into a written form around 200 CE called the Mishnah. The third is the secret law called the Kabbalah. The secrets of the Kabbalah are based on the Torah and were written down around 200 CE. The main books of the Kabbalah are the Zohar and the Book of Creation.

Many of Yeshua's statements have Kabbalah undertones. Yeshua would have known the Kabbalah. Paul would have known the basics, at least, of the Kabbalah because of his religious education and training.

There are Kabbalistic ideas in the Gospels and Paul's letters. Kabbalistic verses will be highlighted in the chapters of the letters.

Methodology

The methodology employed is to use "Ancient Bible Study Methods" integrated with Jesus's day's customs and culture to examine the Hebrew and Christian Scriptures, thus gathering a more in-depth understanding by learning the Scriptures in the way the people of Jesus's day did.

I have titled the methodology of analyzing a passage of Scripture in a Hebraic manner the "Process of Discovery." The author developed this methodology, which combines various linguistic and cultural understanding areas. There are several sections to the process, and not all the parts apply to every passage of Scripture. The overall result of developing this process is to give the reader a framework for studying the Word in more depth.

The "Process of Discovery" starts with a Scripture passage. An examination of the linguistic structure of the passage is next. The linguistic structure includes parallelism, chiastic structures, and repetition. Formatting the passage in its linguistic form allows the reader to visualize what the first-century CE listener was hearing. Their corresponding sections label the chiasms, for example, A, B, C, B', A.' Not all passages of the Scriptures have a poetic form.

The next step is to "question the narrative." The narrative process of questioning the narrative assumes the reader knows nothing about the passage. Therefore, the questions go from simple to complex. The next task is to identify any linguistic patterns. Linguistic patterns include, but are not limited to, irony, simile, metaphor, symbolism, idioms, hyperbole, figurative language, personification, and allegory.

A review of any translation inconsistencies discovered between the English NAU version and Hebrew or Greek versions is done. Sometimes, a Hebrew or Greek word is translated in more than one way. Inconsistencies also can be created by the translation committee, which may have decided to use traditional language instead of the actual translation. The decision of the translation committee is in the Preface or Introduction to the Bible. Perhaps some of the inconsistencies were intentionally added to convey some deeper meaning. An examination of every discrepancy is done.

The passage is analyzed for any echoes of the Hebrew Scriptures in the Christian Scriptures. An echo occurs using a passage from the Hebrew Scriptures in the Christian Scriptures.[3] Also, echoes are found when Torah (Genesis through Deuteronomy) passages are used in other Hebrew Bible books. Cross-references in the Scripture are references from one verse to another verse, which can help the reader understand the verse.

The names of persons mentioned in the passage are listed. Many Hebrew names have meaning and may be associated with places or actions. Jewish parents used to name their children based on what they felt God had in store for their children. An example is Abraham, whose original name was Abram and was changed to mean eternal father (God changed Abram's name to Abraham, indicating a function he was to perform). When the Hebrew Bible gives names, many occurrences mean something unique. The same importance can occur for the names of places. The time it takes to travel between locations can supply insight into the event.

---

[3] Mitzvot are the 613 commandments found in the Torah that please God. There are positive and negative commandments. The list was first development by Maimonides. The full list can be found at: ttp://www.jewfaq.org/613.htm.

Keyphrases are identified in verses when they are essential to understanding that passage. There are no rules for selecting the keywords. Searching for other occurrences of the keywords in Scripture in concordance is necessary to understand the Word's usage; this must be done in either Hebrew or Greek, not in English. A classic Hebraic approach is to find the usage of a word in the Scripture by finding other verses that contain the Word. The usage of a word in its original language is discovered by searching the Scripture in the language of the Word. Verses that contain the Word are identified, and a pattern for the usage of the Word is discovered. Each verse is examined to see what the usage of the Word is, which may reveal a model for the Word's usage. The first usage of the Word in the Scripture, primarily if used in the Torah, is essential for Hebrew words. The Christian Scriptures are used for Greek words to determine the Word usage in the Scripture. Sometimes, finding the equivalent Greek Word in the Septuagint can be beneficial as analyzing its Hebrew usage.

The Rules of Hillel are used when applicable. Hillel was a Torah scholar who lived shortly before Jesus' day. Hillel developed several rules for Torah students to interpret the Scriptures, which refer to halachic Midrash. In several cases, these rules are helpful in the analysis of the Scripture.

The cultural implications from the writing period are done after the linguistic analysis is completed. The culture is crucial because it is not explicitly referenced in the biblical narratives, as indicated earlier.

From the linguistic analysis and the cultural understanding, it is possible to obtain a deeper meaning of the Scripture beyond the plain text's literal meaning. That is what the listeners of Jesus's time were doing. They put linguistics and culture together without even having to contemplate it.

The analysis will lead to findings explaining the passage's meaning in Jesus's day. Most of the time, the Hebraic analysis leads to the desire for more in-depth analysis to fully understand what Jesus was talking about or what was happening to Him. Whatever the result, a new, more in-depth understanding of the Scripture is obtained.

The components of the Process of Discovery are:

Language

Process of Discovery

Linguistics Section

Linguistic Structure

Discussion

Questioning the Passage

Verse Comparison of citations or proof text

Translation Inconsistencies

Biblical Personalities

Biblical Locations

Phrase Study

Only the applicable sections are included in this document.

Introduction to the Letter – 1 Timothy

Timothy was probably an overseer (bishop) of the congregations that Paul started or converted in Asia Minor. There is a scholarly debate as to whether the two letters to Timothy were written by Paul or from the School of Paull toward the end of the first century. Since Paul died in 62 CE if the letter is from the later part of the century then it could not have been written by Paul. Students of Paul were allowed in the Greek culture to sign a letter in the name of the founder of the school. It was the belief that the students were acting in accordance with their teacher.

Timothy lived at Lystra in Southeast Asia minor. Church tradition says that he was converted to Christianity as a part of the traveling missionary work from either Paul or a student of Paul. Timothy's father was a Gentile and his mother was a Jewish follower of Yeshua.[4]

The theme of the letter is discipline and good conduct. Timothy is cautioned against hasty judgment of people. He was also told to be careful who he made elders, and deacons.

---

[4] 1. Rocco A. Errico and George M. Lamsa, *Aramaic Light on Galatians through Hebrews: A Commentary Based on Aramaic, the Language of Jesus, and Ancient near Eastern Customs* (Smyma, GA: Noohra Foundation, 2005).

Chapter One

Language

Peshitta	New American Standard 1995
1Tim. 1:1 Paul, a legate of Jesus the Messiah, by the command of God our life-giver, and of the Messiah, Jesus our hope; ² to Timothy, [my] true son in the faith: grace and mercy and peace, from God our Father, and the Messiah, Jesus our Lord. ³ When I was going into Macedonia, I requested thee to remain at Ephesus, and to charge certain persons not to teach different doctrines; ⁴ and not to throw themselves into fables and stories about genealogies, of which there is no end, which produce contention rather than edification in the faith of God. ⁵ Now the end of the command is love, which is from a pure heart, and from a good conscience, and from true faith. ⁶ But from these some have strayed, and have turned aside to vain words; ⁷ because they wished to be teachers of the law, while they understood not what they speak, nor the thing about which they contend. ⁸ Now, we know, that the law is a good thing, if a man conduct himself in it, according to the law, ⁹ he knowing that the law was not established for the righteous, but for the evil, and the rebellious, and the ungodly, and the sinful, and the perverse and for the impure, and for smiters of their fathers and smiters of their mothers, and for murderers, ¹⁰ and for whoremongers, and for copulators with males, and for the stealers of free people, and for liars, and for violators of oaths, and for whatever is contrary to	**1Tim. 1:1** Paul, *^a*an apostle of *^b*Christ Jesus *^c*according to the commandment of *^c*God our Savior, and of *^b*Christ Jesus, *who is* our *^d*hope, **1Tim. 1:2** To *^a*Timothy, *^amy* true child in *the* faith: *^b*Grace, mercy *and* peace from God the Father and *^c*Christ Jesus our Lord. **1Tim. 1:3** As I urged you *¹*upon my departure for *^a*Macedonia, *²*remain on at *^b*Ephesus so that you may instruct certain men not to *^c*teach strange doctrines, ⁴ nor to *¹*pay attention to *^a*myths and endless *^b*genealogies, which give rise to mere *^c*speculation rather than *^dfurthering ²*the administration of God which is by faith. ⁵ But the goal of our *^{1a}*instruction is love *^b*from a pure heart and a *^c*good conscience and a sincere *^d*faith. ⁶ For some men, straying from these things, have turned aside to *^a*fruitless discussion, ⁷ *^a*wanting to be *^b*teachers of the Law, even though they do not understand either what they are saying or the matters about which they make confident assertions. **1Tim. 1:8** But we know that *^a*the Law is good, if one uses it lawfully, ⁹ realizing the fact that *^a*law is not made for a righteous person, but for those who are lawless and *^b*rebellious, for the *^c*ungodly and sinners, for the unholy and *^d*profane,

sound doctrine, **11** [namely] that of the glorious gospel of the blessed God, with which I am intrusted. **12** And I thank him who strengthened me, [even] our Lord Jesus the Messiah; who accounted me faithful, and appointed me to his ministry; **13** me [I say], who before was a blasphemer, and a persecutor, and a reviler; but I obtained mercy, because I did it while ignorant and without faith. **14** And in me the grace of our Lord abounded, and faith and love, which is in Jesus the Messiah. **15** Faithful is the declaration, and worthy to be received, that Jesus the Messiah came into the world to give life to sinners, of whom I was the primary. **16** But for this cause had he mercy on me, that in me first Jesus the Messiah might display all his long suffering, for an example to them who were to believe on him unto life eternal. **17** And to the king eternal, incorruptible, and invisible, the sole God, be honor and glory for ever and ever! Amen. **18** This injunction I commit to thee, my son Timothy, according to the former predictions concerning thee, that in them thou mightest war this good warfare, **19** in faith and a good conscience; for they who have repudiated this, have become destitute of faith; **20** like Hymeneus and Alexander, whom I have delivered up to Satan, that they may learn not to be blasphemers.

for those who kill their fathers or mothers, for murderers **10** [1]and [2a]immoral men [1]and [b]homosexuals [1]and [c]kidnappers [1]and [d]liars [1]and [e]perjurers, and whatever else is contrary to [f]sound teaching, **11** according to [a]the glorious gospel of [b]the blessed God, with which I have been [c]entrusted.

1Tim. 1:12 I thank [a]Christ Jesus our Lord, who has [b]strengthened me, because He considered me faithful, [c]putting me into service, **13** even though I was formerly a blasphemer and a [a]persecutor and a violent aggressor. Yet I was [b]shown mercy because [c]I acted ignorantly in unbelief; **14** and the [a]grace of our Lord was more than abundant, with the [b]faith and love which are *found* in Christ Jesus. **15** [a]It is a trustworthy statement, deserving full acceptance, that [b]Christ Jesus came into the world to [c]save sinners, among whom [d]I am foremost *of all*. **16** Yet for this reason I [a]found mercy, so that in me as the foremost, Jesus Christ might [b]demonstrate His perfect patience as an example for those [1]who would believe in Him for eternal life. **17** Now to the [a]King [1]eternal, [b]immortal, [c]invisible, the [d]only God, [e]be honor and glory [2]forever and ever. Amen.

1Tim. 1:18 This [a]command I entrust to you, Timothy, [b]*my* [1]son, in accordance with the [c]prophecies previously made concerning you, that by them you [d]fight the good fight, **19** keeping [a]faith and a good conscience, which some have rejected and suffered shipwreck in regard to [1b]their faith. **20** [1]Among these are [a]Hymenaeus and [b]Alexander, whom I have [c]handed over to

	Satan, so that they will be [d]taught not to blaspheme.

1Timothy 1:1
[a]2 Cor 1:1
[b]1 Tim 1:12
[c]Titus 1:3
[d]Col 1:27

1Timothy 1:2
[a]2 Tim 1:2
[b]Rom 1:7; 2 Tim 1:2; Titus 1:4
[c]1 Tim 1:12

1Timothy 1:3
[1]Lit *while going to*
[2]Lit *to remain*
[a]Rom 15:26
[b]Acts 18:19
[c]Rom 16:17; 2 Cor 11:4; Gal 1:6f; 1 Tim 6:3

1Timothy 1:4
[1]Or *occupy themselves with*
[2]Lit *God's provision*
[a]1 Tim 4:7; 2 Tim 4:4; Titus 1:14; 2 Pet 1:16
[b]Titus 3:9
[c]2 Tim 2:23
[d]Eph 3:2

1Timothy 1:5
[1]Lit *commandment*
[a]1 Tim 1:18
[b]2 Tim 2:22
[c]1 Tim 1:19; 3:9; 2 Tim 1:3; 1 Pet 3:16, 21
[d]2 Tim 1:5

1Timothy 1:6
[a]Titus 1:10

1Timothy 1:7

[a]James 3:1
[b]Luke 2:46

1Timothy 1:8
[a]Rom 7:12, 16

1Timothy 1:9
[a]Gal 5:23
[b]Titus 1:6, 10
[c]1 Pet 4:18; Jude 15
[d]1 Tim 4:7; 6:20; Heb 12:16

1Timothy 1:10
[1]Lit *for*
[2]Or *fornicators*
[a]1 Cor 6:9
[b]Lev 18:22
[c]Ex 21:16; Rev 18:13
[d]Rev 21:8, 27; 22:15
[e]Matt 5:33
[f]1 Tim 4:6; 6:3; 2 Tim 4:3; Titus 1:9, 13; 2:1, 2

1Timothy 1:11
[a]2 Cor 4:4
[b]1 Tim 6:15
[c]Gal 2:7

1Timothy 1:12
[a]Gal 3:26
[b]Acts 9:22; Phil 4:13; 2 Tim 4:17
[c]Acts 9:15

1Timothy 1:13
[a]Acts 8:3
[b]1 Cor 7:25
[c]Acts 26:9

1Timothy 1:14
[a]Rom 5:20; 1 Cor 3:10; 2 Cor 4:15; Gal 1:13-16
[b]1 Thess 1:3; 1 Tim 2:15; 4:12; 6:11; 2 Tim 1:13; 2:22; Titus 2:2

1Timothy 1:15
[a]1 Tim 3:1; 4:9; 2 Tim 2:11; Titus 3:8
[b]Mark 2:17; Luke 15:2ff; 19:10
[c]Rom 11:14
[d]1 Cor 15:9; Eph 3:8

1Timothy 1:16
[1]Or *destined to*
[a]1 Cor 7:25; 1 Tim 1:13
[b]Eph 2:7

1Timothy 1:17
[1]Lit *of the ages*
[2]Lit *to the ages of the ages*
[a]Rev 15:3
[b]1 Tim 6:16
[c]Col 1:15
[d]John 5:44; 1 Tim 6:15; Jude 25
[e]Rom 2:7, 10; 11:36; Heb 2:7

1Timothy 1:18
[1]Or *child*
[a]1 Tim 1:5
[b]1 Tim 1:2
[c]1 Tim 4:14
[d]2 Cor 10:4; 1 Tim 6:12; 2 Tim 2:3f; 4:7

1Timothy 1:19
[1]Lit *the*
[a]1 Tim 1:5
[b]1 Tim 6:12, 21; 2 Tim 2:18

1Timothy 1:20
[1]Lit *Of*
[a]2 Tim 2:17
[b]2 Tim 4:14
[c]1 Cor 5:5
[d]1 Cor 11:32; Heb 12:5ff

Koine Greek

1Tim. 1:0 ΠΡΟΣ ΤΙΜΟΘΕΟΝ Α

1Tim. 1:1 Παυλος αποστολος Χριστου Ιησου κατ' επιταγην θεου σωτηρος ημων και Χριστου Ιησου της ελπιδος ημων ² Τιμοθεω γνησιω τεκνω εν πιστει, χαρις ελεος ειρηνη απο θεου πατρος και Χριστου Ιησου του κυριου ημων.

1Tim. 1:3 Καθως παρεκαλεσα σε προσμειναι εν Εφεσω πορευομενος εις Μακεδονιαν, ινα παραγγειλης τισιν μη ετεροδιδασκαλειν ⁴ μηδε προσεχειν μυθοις και γενεαλογιαις απεραντοις, αιτινες εκζητησεις παρεχουσιν μαλλον η οικονομιαν θεου την εν πιστει. ⁵ το δε τελος της παραγγελιας εστιν αγαπη εκ καθαρας καρδιας και συνειδησεως αγαθης και πιστεως ανυποκριτου, ⁶ ων τινες αστοχησαντες εξετραπησαν εις ματαιολογιαν ⁷ θελοντες ειναι νομοδιδασκαλοι, μη νοουντες μητε α λεγουσιν μητε περι τινων διαβεβαιουνται. ⁸ Οιδαμεν δε οτι καλος ο νομος, εαν τις αυτω νομιμως χρηται, ⁹ ειδως τουτο, οτι δικαιω νομος ου κειται, ανομοις δε και ανυποτακτοις, ασεβεσιν και αμαρτωλοις, ανοσιοις και βεβηλοις, πατρολωαις και μητρολωαις, ανδροφονοις ¹⁰ πορνοις αρσενοκοιταις ανδραποδισταις ψευσταις επιορκοις, και ει τι ετερον τη υγιαινουση διδασκαλια αντικειται ¹¹ κατα το ευαγγελιον της δοξης του μακαριου θεου, ο επιστευθην εγω.

1Tim. 1:12 Χαριν εχω τω ενδυναμωσαντι με Χριστω Ιησου τω κυριω ημων, οτι πιστον με ηγησατο θεμενος εις διακονιαν ¹³ το προτερον οντα βλασφημον και διωκτην και υβριστην, αλλ' ηλεηθην, οτι αγνοων εποιησα εν απιστια· ¹⁴ υπερεπλεονασεν δε η χαρις του κυριου ημων μετα πιστεως και αγαπης της εν Χριστω Ιησου. ¹⁵ πιστος ο λογος και πασης αποδοχης αξιος, οτι Χριστος Ιησους ηλθεν εις τον κοσμον αμαρτωλους σωσαι, ων πρωτος ειμι εγω. ¹⁶ αλλα δια τουτο ηλεηθην, ινα εν εμοι πρωτω ενδειξηται Χριστος Ιησους την απασαν μακροθυμιαν προς υποτυπωσιν των μελλοντων πιστευειν επ' αυτω εις ζωην αιωνιον. ¹⁷ Τω δε βασιλει των αιωνων, αφθαρτω αορατω μονω θεω, τιμη και δοξα εις τους αιωνας των αιωνων, αμην.

1Tim. 1:18 Ταυτην την παραγγελιαν παρατιθεμαι σοι, τεκνον Τιμοθεε, κατα τας προαγουσας επι σε προφητειας, ινα στρατευη εν αυταις την καλην στρατειαν ¹⁹ εχων πιστιν και αγαθην συνειδησιν, ην τινες απωσαμενοι περι την πιστιν εναυαγησαν, ²⁰ ων εστιν Υμεναιος και Αλεξανδρος, ους παρεδωκα τω σατανα, ινα παιδευθωσιν μη βλασφημειν.

Language

  Process of Discovery

    Linguistics Section

    Linguistic Structure

[Introduction] 1Tim. 1:1   Paul, *a*an apostle of *b*Christ Jesus *c*according to the commandment of *c*God our Savior, and of *b*Christ Jesus, *who is* our *d*hope, **1Tim. 1:2**   To *a*Timothy, *a*my true child in *the* faith: *b*Grace, mercy *and* peace from God the Father and *c*Christ Jesus our Lord.

[Exhortations] 1Tim. 1:3   As I urged you [1]upon my departure for *a*Macedonia, [2]remain on at *b*Ephesus so that you may instruct certain men not to *c*teach strange doctrines, [4] nor to [1]pay attention to *a*myths and endless *b*genealogies, which give rise to mere *c*speculation rather than *d furthering* [2]the administration of God which is by faith. [5] But the goal of our [1a]instruction is love *b*from a pure heart and a *c*good conscience and a sincere *d*faith. [6] For some men, straying from these things, have turned aside to *a*fruitless discussion, [7] *a*wanting to be *b*teachers of the Law, even though they do not understand either what they are saying or the matters about which they make confident assertions. **1Tim. 1:8**   But we know that *a*the Law is good, if one uses it lawfully, [9] realizing the fact that *a*law is not made for a righteous person, but for those who are lawless and *b*rebellious, for the *c*ungodly and sinners, for the unholy and *d*profane, for those who kill their fathers or mothers, for murderers [10] [1]and [2a]immoral men [1]and *b*homosexuals [1]and *c*kidnappers [1]and *d*liars [1]and *e*perjurers, and whatever else is contrary to *f*sound teaching, [11] according to *a*the glorious gospel of *b*the blessed God, with which I have been *c*entrusted.

[Thanksgiving] 1Tim. 1:12   I thank *a*Christ Jesus our Lord, who has *b*strengthened me, because He considered me faithful, *c*putting me into service, [13] even though I was formerly a blasphemer and a *a*persecutor and a violent aggressor. Yet I was *b*shown mercy because *c*I acted ignorantly in unbelief; [14] and the *a*grace of our Lord was more than abundant, with the *b*faith and love which are *found* in Christ Jesus. [15] *a*It is a trustworthy statement, deserving full acceptance, that *b*Christ Jesus came into the world to *c*save sinners, among whom *d*I am foremost *of all.* [16] Yet for this reason I *a*found mercy, so that in me as the foremost, Jesus Christ might *b*demonstrate His perfect patience as an example for those [1]who would believe in Him for eternal life. [17] Now to the *a*King [1]eternal, *b*immortal, *c*invisible, the *d*only God, *e be* honor and glory [2]forever and ever. Amen.

[Closing statement] 1Tim. 1:18   This *a*command I entrust to you, Timothy, *b*my [1]son, in accordance with the *c*prophecies previously made concerning you, that by them you

[d]fight the good fight, [19] keeping [a]faith and a good conscience, which some have rejected and suffered shipwreck in regard to [1b]their faith. [20] [1]Among these are [a]Hymenaeus and [b]Alexander, whom I have [c]handed over to Satan, so that they will be [d]taught not to blaspheme.

Discussion

In Paul's usual style, he says "hello" and then gives condemnations and exhortations.

Questioning the Passage

1. What is the difference between life-giver and savior in verse one?

   Church tradition has determined that Paul said that God is our savior and since Yeshua is a part of the Trinity, then all three parts are our savior. "God our savior" appears in this letter, Titus and Jude. A non-tradition view is that it is the LORD (God) who can offer forgiveness for sin. That was an acceptance position of the Jewish population. They accused Yeshua of saying that he could forgive sin. Only the LORD could do that. Therefore, in this verse, the author must have been Jewish or well acquainted with the Jewish position of forgiveness. Since the Trinity doctrine was not formalized until at least one-hundred years later, people would regard the idea of how salvation worked as new and unknown. Also, we cannot attribute this phrase to Paul's theological position since it does not appear in any of his accepted letters. Since Yeshua did not cause a revolution, as the Messianic tradition of the day believed, then Yeshua brought a prophetic message from the LORD to the people. That message was to get salvation and thus the forgiveness of sin on needed to follow the two great commandments: love God and love neighbor. The LORD will forgive the sins of people who follow the commandment as spelled out in the Torah.

2. What does it mean that Yeshua is our hope? (v. 1)

"The promise of hope was one of Christianity's most outstanding features in a world in which hope had little place. Pessimism dominated popular belief. The philosophers had dismissed the Olympian gods but had not replaced them with an alternative that provided hope for people. Most could see only the fear and senselessness of chance and the arbitrariness and finality of fate. Stoicism, perhaps the most influential philosophy among the cultured in the first century A.D., taught an apathetic determinism in which individual choice and freedom were absent; one must simply accept whatever fate decides. K. A. Kitchen cites the epitaph "I am of good courage, I who was not, and became, and now am not. I do not grieve" (*ISBE* 2:753). Magic and superstition also abounded. An example of the futility of the times is illustrated by the magical incantation to be used when approached by an unfriendly god: "Lay at once your right [fore-]finger upon your mouth and say, 'Silence! Silence! Silence!' (a symbol of the living, incorruptible god). 'Guard me, Silence!' Then whistle long, then sneeze, and say … and then you will see the gods looking graciously upon you" ("A Mithras Liturgy," in Barrett, *New Testament Background,* 132). Barrett omits what the person is to say, which A. Dieterich (Eine Mithrasliturgie [Leipzig: Teubner, 1903] 2–15) shows to be a conglomeration of sounds that appears to be gibberish. The world was without "hope and without God" (Eph 2:12; cf. 1 Thess 4:13). But "when the time had fully come, God sent forth his Son" (Gal 4:4) so that the indwelling Christ could become "the hope of glory" (Col 1:27). The world was without hope; the message that Jesus is "our hope" (1 Tim 1:1) stood out like a shining beacon in a dark world. For an excellent description of the hopelessness of the ancient world, see Angus, *Environment of Early Christianity;* see also Lohse, *New Testament Environment,* 226–32; R. Bultmann and K. H. Rengstorf, *TDNT* 2:517–33; E. Hoffmann, NIDNTT 2:238–44; K. A. Kitchen, *ISBE* 2:751–55.[5]"

3. What does it mean to be a true child in faith? (v. 2)

    A child in the faith is a person who was new to the faith and thus did not understand all the aspects of the new religion. Being a child is a metaphor for someone who knew to the new way of thinking. Paul was extremely egocentric. Therefore, he believed he was the expert authority and everyone else were to be like children and learn only from him the ways of Yeshua and the faith.

4. What are these different (strange) doctrines? (v. 3)

    The strange doctrines were anything that did not match what Paul told the churches to believe. When Paul converted a Mithras house church, he allowed them to keep their doctrines and rituals with one change. That change was that Mithras was not their god. It was Yeshua who was their God, or at least a part of God, in the same way that Mithras was the son of god. Paul considered anything that did not match up with the converted Mithras doctrine a false doctrine and was not to be followed.

5. What genealogy is being referred to in verse four?

    "*Myth* and *genealogy* are often joined in Greek literature. The scarcity of the pair in Scripture outside the PE is explained by the fact that the heresy had not arisen until the end of Paul's life. Previous to the Ephesian situation, the Judaizing influence showed itself in other ways. In *Introduction,* "The Ephesian Heresy," the background of the "myths and genealogies" is analyzed, and it is argued that they

---

[5] Mounce, W. D. (2000). *Pastoral Epistles* (Vol. 46, p. 7). Word, Incorporated.

are Jewish with some Hellenistic/gnostic elements. This conclusion is largely based on this verse and other similar statements (Titus 1:14). The Jewish element accounts for the misunderstanding of the law (1:7, 8–11) and the quarrels about it (Titus 3:9)."[6]

6. What are the fables (myths) that are being referred to? (v. 4)

   Fables are traditional teachings that are passed down and shared, especially among the uneducated. Paul converted Mithras House Churches, changing the deity from Mithras to the Yeshua of Nazareth. The proof of this is that 90% of Christian rituals and original doctrine were all from the Mithras Cult. There would be members of the congregation who were still semi-loyal to Mithras. Their stories about Mithras would be the fables that this letter is referring to.

7. What have some people turned toward? (v. 6 & 7)

   This is another mention of the different ways Christianity was practiced in its early years. Different forms of Christianity emerged in the 2nd and 3rd centuries CE. Paul strongly believed that only his version was correct. Therefore, to follow one of those other expressions was not wise. It would be interesting to ask Paul what he would think about the many expressions of Christianity today. There are over 1,000 denominations and it is growing with the independent church movement.

---

[6] Mounce, W. D. (2000). *Pastoral Epistles* (Vol. 46, p. 21). Word, Incorporated.

8. What is the Law in verse nine?

The Law is a reference to the Torah.

9. What is the legitimate usage of the Law? (v. 9 – 11)

Paul used the Law to stop congregation members from doing things he thought were against God's will. There were some things in the Mithras cult that Paul had to outlaw in his converted house churches. It is interesting that Paul says that the Law (the Torah) to rid the congregation of the persons listed in verses nine through eleven.

10. Why is the Law not for the righteous person? (v. 9)

A righteous person does not violate the Torah Laws. This person is deeply connected to the LORD that their soul will not allow their flesh to take control and sin against the LORD. The Law is unnecessary for such a pious person. The rest of humanity will act like humans do. They will sin against the LORD from time to time. It is a part of the freewill that the LORD gives to humanity. Therefore, the Torah has forgiveness built into it.

11. What is the grace of the LORD? (v. 14)

It is the LORD's favor and kindness to us. When the LORD forgives a person for their sin it is said that the LORD's grace is upon them.

12. What are the prophecies mentioned in verse eighteen?

Paul believed he was told through Yeshua that Timothy would become a loyal follower of Yeshua and in Paul's manner. Paul commended Timothy for following through with his loyalty to Paul's definition of Christianity.

13. What is the meaning of "fight the good fight?" (v. 18)

Paul expected Timothy would remain loyal to Paul's form of Christianity no matter what the outside pressures would be. Those pressures were from other expressions of Christianity, Jewish persons, and the Roman authorities. We usually attribute the good fight to fighting against idolatry, pagan teachings and customs that were undermining Christianity's growth.

14. What does it mean to suffer a shipwreck (destitute) regarding faith? (v. 19)

This is another opportunity for Paul to tell the congregation that he suffered for the message of the Gospel, his message of what the Gospel means. This is a simple egocentric remark about Paul.

15. How did Paul receive the power to turn souls over to Satan? (v. 20)

"Whom I have delivered to Satan" means "I have let them suffer in their own devices so that they may learn their lesson." A modern equivalent is "Give them enough rope and they will hand themselves. Sometimes it is better to let a person suffer by their own actions than to correct them.

16. What happened to forgiveness and repentance in verse twenty?

Clearly, the idea of forgiveness and repentance could not anyone who disagreed with Paul.

Biblical Personalities

1. Hymenaeus – "Hymenaeus (fl. 50–65, 1 Timothy 1:20, 2 Timothy 2:17) was an early Christian from Ephesus, an opponent of the apostle Paul, who associates him with Alexander and Philetus."[7]

2. Alexander – "Hymenaeus and Alexander were men in the early church in Ephesus who had "suffered shipwreck with regard to the faith" and so were "handed over to Satan" by the apostle Paul (1 Timothy 1:19–20). Hymenaeus and Alexander are thus examples of those who reject the true doctrine and follow the false. Later, Hymenaeus is mentioned with Philetus, another false teacher (2 Timothy 2:17). An opponent of Paul named Alexander the metalworker is mentioned in 2 Timothy 4:15–16, but whether or not this is the same Alexander mentioned in 1 Timothy 1:19 is unknown."[8]

Culture Section

Discussion

Fables were circulated teachings based on traditions that had been handed down through the centuries. The newly converted Mithras Churches would have members that hung onto the "old thinking" even though they accepted that Yeshua of Nazareth is the true God, and that Mithras was not. Fables would also come to the congregation through people who believed in any of the competing beliefs. The strongest group were the Gnostic Christians. This group formed in northern Egypt after Yeshua's death. They believed that Yeshua brought back to us the secret Torah that Moses received on Mount Sinai and had been lost. The

---

[7] 1. "Hymenaeus (Biblical Figure)," Wikipedia, September 3, 2023, https://en.wikipedia.org/wiki/Hymenaeus_(biblical_figure).
[8] 1. GotQuestions.org, "Home," GotQuestions.org, June 7, 2016, https://www.gotquestions.org/Hymenaeus-and-Alexander.html.

truth was the way to enter heaven was to love God and love neighbor. Yeshua's death, according to the Gnostics, was because he brought the message. Salvation comes from following these two commandments. In the Gospels these two commandments are called the Two Great Commandments.

There would have been some competition from the Jewish converts. They would have very different views than the Mithras converts. There is a warning not to allow Jewish ideas about the Messiah change Paul's definition.

Paul's view of God became the same as Yeshua preached. The LORD is like a loving Father who constantly forgives us for our transgressions.[9] There is a Midrash story that the Spirit of the Torah came to the LORD and asked that humanity not be created. The Torah's reason was that humanity was going to sin against the LORD. The LORD's response was that forgiveness was written into the parchment of the Torah. The Zohar (the Secret work) says that creation was done through Elohim, which is the part of the LORD that represents love and mercy. There are very few sins that the LORD will not offer forgiveness for. The LORD is happiest when believers return to the ways of faith, truth and justice.

Thoughts

This chapter is another example that Paul was most concerned that his views of what Yeshua's life was about might be overturned by people from other Christian expressions. He ensures that Timothy is aware of these other expressions and how

---

[9] 1. Rocco A. Errico and George M. Lamsa, *Aramaic Light on Galatians through Hebrews: A Commentary Based on Aramaic, the Language of Jesus, and Ancient near Eastern Customs* (Smyrna, GA: Noohra Foundation, 2005).

wrong they are. It is interesting that Paul does not like the Law (the Torah) in other letters but here he uses the Torah to tell Timothy who should be ejected from the congregation. An interesting question is: Where is grace and mercy in Paul's understanding of Yeshua's words?

Chapter Two

Language

Peshitta	New American Standard 1995
1Timothy 2:1 I exhort thee, therefore, first of all, that thou present to God supplication, and prayer, and intercession, and thanksgiving, for all men: **2** for kings and magistrates, that we may dwell in a quiet and tranquil habitation, with all reverence for God, and with purity. **3** For this is good and acceptable before God our life-giver; **4** who would have all men live, and be converted to the knowledge of the truth. **5** For God is one; and the mediator between God and men is one, [namely] the man Jesus the Messiah; **6** who gave himself a ransom for every man; a testimony that arrived in due time, **7** of which I am constituted a herald and legate. I speak the truth, and do not lie, for I am the teacher of the Gentiles in the belief of the truth. **8** I desire therefore, that men may pray in every place, while they lift up their hands with purity, without wrath, and without disputations. **9** So also, that women [appear] in a chaste fashion of dress; and that their adorning be with modesty and chastity; not with curls, or with gold, or with pearls, or with splendid robes; **10** but with good works, as becometh women who profess reverence for God. **11** Let a woman learn in silence, with all submission: **12** for I do not allow a woman to teach, or to be assuming over the man; but let her remain in stillness. **13**	**Timothy 2:1** First of all, then, I urge that [a]entreaties *and* prayers, petitions *and* thanksgivings, be made on behalf of all men, **2** [a]for kings and all who are in [1]authority, so that we may lead a tranquil and quiet life in all godliness and [2]dignity. **3** This is good and acceptable in the sight of [a]God our Savior, **4** [a]who desires all men to be [b]saved and to [c]come to the [1]knowledge of the truth. **5** For there is [a]one God, *and* [b]one mediator also between God and men, *the* [c]man Christ Jesus, **6** who [a]gave Himself as a ransom for all, the [b]testimony [1]*given* at [2c]the proper time. **7** [a]For this I was appointed a [1]preacher and [b]an apostle (I am telling the truth, I am not lying) as a teacher of [d]the Gentiles in faith and truth. **1Timothy 2:8** Therefore [a]I want the men [b]in every place to pray, [c]lifting up [d]holy hands, without wrath and dissension. **9** Likewise, *I want* [a]women to adorn themselves with proper clothing, [1]modestly and discreetly, not with braided hair and gold or pearls or costly garments, **10** but rather by means of good works, as is proper for women making a claim to godliness. **11** [a]A woman must quietly receive instruction with entire submissiveness. **12** [a]But I do not allow a woman to teach or exercise authority

For Adam was first formed, and then Eve. **14** And Adam was not seduced, but the woman was seduced and transgressed the command. **15** Yet she shall live by means of her children, if they continue in the faith, and in love, and in sanctity, and in chastity.

over a man, but to remain quiet. **13** *a*For it was Adam who was first [1]created, *and* then Eve. **14** And *it was* not Adam *who* was deceived, but *a*the woman being deceived, [1]fell into transgression. **15** But *women* will be [1]preserved through the bearing of children if they continue in *a*faith and love and sanctity with [2]self-restraint.

1Timothy 2:1
[a]Eph 6:18

1Timothy 2:2
[1]Or *a high position*
[2]Or *seriousness*
[a]Ezra 6:10; Rom 13:1

1Timothy 2:3
[a]Luke 1:47; 1 Tim 1:1; 4:10

1Timothy 2:4
[1]Or *recognition*
[a]Ezek 18:23, 32; John 3:17; 1 Tim 4:10; Titus 2:11; 2 Pet 3:9
[b]Rom 11:14
[c]2 Tim 2:25; 3:7; Titus 1:1; Heb 10:26

1Timothy 2:5
[a]Rom 3:30; 10:12; 1 Cor 8:4
[b]1 Cor 8:6; Gal 3:20
[c]Matt 1:1; Rom 1:3

1Timothy 2:6
[1]Or *to be given*
[2]Lit *its own times*
[a]Matt 20:28; Gal 1:4
[b]1 Cor 1:6
[c]Mark 1:15; Gal 4:4; 1 Tim 6:15; Titus 1:3

1Timothy 2:7
[1]Or *herald*
[a]Eph 3:8; 1 Tim 1:11; 2 Tim 1:11
[b]1 Cor 9:1
[c]Rom 9:1
[d]Acts 9:15

1Timothy 2:8

^aPhil 1:12; 1 Tim 5:14; Titus 3:8
^bJohn 4:21; 1 Cor 1:2; 2 Cor 2:14; 1 Thess 1:8
^cPs 63:4; Luke 24:50
^dPs 24:4; James 4:8

1Timothy 2:9
[1]Lit *with modesty*
[a]1 Pet 3:3

1Timothy 2:11
[a]1 Cor 14:34; Titus 2:5

1Timothy 2:12
[a]1 Cor 14:34; Titus 2:5

1Timothy 2:13
[1]Or *formed*
[a]Gen 2:7, 22; 3:16; 1 Cor 11:8ff

1Timothy 2:14
[1]Lit *has come*
[a]Gen 3:6, 13; 2 Cor 11:3

1Timothy 2:15
[1]Lit *saved*
[2]Or *discretion*
[a]1 Tim 1:14

1Timothy 2:1 Παρακαλῶ οὖν πρῶτον πάντων ποιεῖσθαι δεήσεις, προσευχάς, ἐντεύξεις, εὐχαριστίας, ὑπὲρ πάντων ἀνθρώπων· **2** ὑπὲρ βασιλέων καὶ πάντων τῶν ἐν ὑπεροχῇ ὄντων, ἵνα ἤρεμον καὶ ἡσύχιον βίον διάγωμεν ἐν πάσῃ εὐσεβείᾳ καὶ σεμνοτητι. **3** τοῦτο γὰρ καλὸν καὶ ἀπόδεκτον ἐνώπιον τοῦ σωτῆρος ἡμῶν θεοῦ, **4** ὃς πάντας ἀνθρώπους θέλει σωθῆναι καὶ εἰς ἐπίγνωσιν ἀληθείας ἐλθεῖν. **5** Εἷς γὰρ θεός, εἷς καὶ μεσίτης θεοῦ καὶ ἀνθρώπων, ἄνθρωπος χριστὸς Ἰησοῦς, **6** ὁ δοὺς ἑαυτὸν ἀντίλυτρον ὑπὲρ πάντων, τὸ μαρτύριον καιροῖς ἰδίοις, **7** εἰς ὃ ἐτέθην ἐγὼ κῆρυξ καὶ ἀπόστολος· ἀλήθειαν λέγω ἐν χριστῷ, οὐ ψεύδομαι· διδάσκαλος ἐθνῶν ἐν πίστει καὶ ἀληθείᾳ.

1Timothy 2:8 Βούλομαι οὖν προσεύχεσθαι τοὺς ἄνδρας ἐν παντὶ τόπῳ, ἐπαίροντας ὁσίους χεῖρας, χωρὶς ὀργῆς καὶ διαλογισμοῦ. **9** Ὡσαύτως καὶ τὰς γυναῖκας ἐν καταστολῇ κοσμίῳ, μετὰ αἰδοῦς καὶ σωφροσύνης, κοσμεῖν ἑαυτάς, μὴ ἐν πλέγμασιν, ἢ χρυσῷ, ἢ μαργαρίταις, ἢ ἱματισμῷ πολυτελεῖ, **10** ἀλλ’ ὃ πρέπει γυναιξὶν ἐπαγγελλομέναις θεοσέβειαν, δι’ ἔργων ἀγαθῶν. **11** Γυνὴ ἐν ἡσυχίᾳ μανθανέτω ἐν πάσῃ ὑποταγῇ. **12** Γυναικὶ δὲ διδάσκειν οὐκ ἐπιτρέπω, οὐδὲ αὐθεντεῖν ἀνδρός, ἀλλ’ εἶναι ἐν ἡσυχίᾳ. **13** Ἀδὰμ γὰρ πρῶτος ἐπλάσθη, εἶτα Εὔα· **14** καὶ Ἀδὰμ οὐκ ἠπατήθη, ἡ δὲ γυνὴ ἀπατηθεῖσα ἐν παραβάσει γέγονεν· **15** σωθήσεται δὲ διὰ τῆς τεκνογονίας, ἐὰν μείνωσιν ἐν πίστει καὶ ἀγάπῃ καὶ ἁγιασμῷ μετὰ σωφροσύνης.

Language

Process of Discovery

Linguistics Section

Linguistic Structure

Timothy 2:1 First of all, then, I urge that *ᵃ*entreaties *and* prayers, petitions *and* thanksgivings, be made on behalf of all men, **2** *ᵃ*for kings and all who are in *¹*authority, so that we may lead a tranquil and quiet life in all godliness and *²*dignity. **3** This is good and acceptable in the sight of *ᵃ*God our Savior, **4** *ᵃ*who desires all men to be *ᵇ*saved and to *ᶜ*come to the *¹*knowledge of the truth. **5** For there is *ᵃ*one God, *and* *ᵇ*one mediator also between God and men, *the ᶜ*man Christ Jesus, **6** who *ᵃ*gave Himself as a ransom for all, the *ᵇ*testimony *¹given* at *²ᶜ*the proper time. **7** *ᵃ*For this I was appointed a *¹*preacher and *ᵇ*an apostle (*ᶜ*I am telling the truth, I am not lying) as a teacher of *ᵈ*the Gentiles in faith and truth. **1Timothy 2:8** Therefore *ᵃ*I want the men *ᵇ*in every place to pray, *ᶜ*lifting up *ᵈ*holy hands, without wrath and dissension.

[Women] 9 Likewise, *I want ᵃ*women to adorn themselves with proper clothing, *¹*modestly and discreetly, not with braided hair and gold or pearls or costly garments, **10** but rather by means of good works, as is proper for women making a claim to godliness. **11** *ᵃ*A woman must quietly receive instruction with entire submissiveness. **12** *ᵃ*But I do not allow a woman to teach or exercise authority over a man, but to remain quiet. **13** *ᵃ*For it was Adam who was first *¹*created, *and* then Eve. **14** And *it was* not Adam *who* was deceived, but *ᵃ*the woman being deceived, *¹*fell into transgression. **15** But *women* will be *¹*preserved through the bearing of children if they continue in *ᵃ*faith and love and sanctity with *²*self-restraint.

Discussion

This is a very difficult chapter to engage with in today's society in the western world. However, it is a part of this epistle, and the church bishops decided in 456 CE that it was to be included in the Bible. During the latter half of the first century CE, the proto-orthodox church was struggling. The church promised that one would have a better life if one believed in Yeshua as the Messiah. It is not known exactly when Yeshua was made by God. By the end of the first century CE, that transition had occurred. The Mithras House churches Paul converted certainly viewed Yeshua as God because he replaced Mithras.

In the Roman Empire during this time period, the only accepted religions were the state sponsored one, Mithras and Judaism. Every other religious expression was placed under the pressure of the government. If a person became a Christian, they would lose their government job as soon as that information became public. Christian churches formed communities for protection.

Early church leaders thought that if Christianity had a leadership structure similar to Rome, the government might be more accepting and persecution would stop. Therefore, a hierarchy that resembled Rome was created. The structure of the Pope was equated to the emperor. The Cardinals became like the Senate and so forth. The next problem was that woman were in key positions inside the church. In the last chapter of the Epistle to Rome, Paul speaks about deacons and names several women as Deacons. Women held several key positions in the churches and had a lot of authority over the workings of the church.

This practice had to be stopped if the church was going to emulate Rome. Therefore, women had to be removed from leadership positions. This chapter is an example of either a reaction to the original letter or it was written after Paul's death. This chapter and other features in the letter do not correspond to Paul's advice in his other letters. Women were very important to the beginnings of the proto-orthodox church and Paul knew it. It is out of place for him to write such a chapter. That is why there is doubt that this was his letter, or this chapter is an add on redaction of the original.

Either way the church used this chapter to push women out of leadership roles and kept them out from a long time. The bishops in 456 CE, being all male, certainly must have enjoyed including this letter in the Bible because it fit their power structure. Once the epistle was canonized it gave the men of the church the "biblical approval" to keep women out of any leadership or education role. There are churches today that still stand by this chapter and keep women out of the leadership roles of their churches.

There are numerous items in the Bible which applied in ancient times that may not apply today. Certainly, this chapter is one of them. A lot also depends on whether you believe that Paul's writings are considered sacred. Paul converted Mithras House churches into Yeshua House churches. His epistles became the cornerstone of the doctrines and beliefs that are maintained today in Christianity. A lot of Paul's commandments do not have the support of the Gospels or even the other biblical writings to support them. It is up to the individual to determine what value can be placed on Paul's letters.

Chapter Three

Language

Peshitta	New American Standard 1995
1Timothy 3:1 It is a faithful saying, that if a man desireth the eldership, he desireth a good work. **2** And an elder ought to be such, that no blame can be found in him; and he should be the husband of one wife, with a vigilant mind, and sober and regular [in his habits], and affectionate to strangers, and instructive; **3** and not a transgressor in regard to wine, and whose hand is not swift to strike; but he should be humble, and not contentious, nor a lover of money; **4** and one that guideth well his own house, and holdeth his children in subjection with all purity. **5** For if he knoweth not how to guide his own house well, how can he guide the church of God. **6** Neither let him be of recent discipleship; lest he be uplifted, and fall into the condemnation of Satan. **7** And there ought to be good testimony of him from those without; lest he fall into reproach and the snare of Satan. **8** And so also the deacons should be pure, and not speak double, nor incline to much wine, nor love base gains; **9** but should hold the mystery of the faith with a pure conscience. **10** And let them be first tried, and then let them serve, if they are without blame. **11** So also should the wives be chaste and of vigilant minds; and they should be faithful in all things; and they should not be slanderers. **12** Let the deacons be such as have each one wife and guide well their children and households.	**1Timothy 3:1** [a]It is a trustworthy statement: if any man aspires to the [b]office of [1]overseer, it is a fine work he desires *to do*. **2** [1a]An overseer, then, must be above reproach, [b]the husband of one wife, [c]temperate, prudent, respectable, [d]hospitable, [e]able to teach, **3** [a]not addicted to wine [1]or pugnacious, but gentle, peaceable, [b]free from the love of money. **4** *He must be* one who [a]manages his own household well, keeping his children under control with all dignity **5** (but if a man does not know how to manage his own household, how will he take care of [a]the church of God?), **6** *and* not a new convert, so that he will not become [a]conceited and fall into the [b]condemnation [1]incurred by the devil. **7** And he must [a]have a good reputation with [b]those outside *the church,* so that he will not fall into reproach and [c]the snare of the devil. **1Timothy 3:8** [a]Deacons likewise *must be* men of dignity, not [1]double-tongued, [2b]or addicted to much wine [2c]or fond of sordid gain, **9** [a]but holding to the mystery of the faith with a clear conscience. **10** [a]These men must also first be tested; then let them serve as deacons if they are beyond reproach. **11** [1]Women *must* likewise *be* dignified, [a]not malicious gossips, but [b]temperate, faithful in all things. **12** [a]Deacons must be [b]husbands of *only* one wife, *and* [1c]good managers of *their* children

13 For they who serve well [as deacons], procure for themselves a good degree, and much boldness in the faith of Jesus the Messiah. **14** These things I write to thee, while hoping soon to come to thee; **15** but if I should delay, that thou mayest know how thou oughtest to conduct thyself in the house of God, which is the church of the living God. The pillar and the foundation of the truth, **16** and truly great, is this mystery of righteousness, which was revealed in the flesh, and justified in the spirit, and seen by angels, and proclaimed among the Gentiles, and believed on in the world, and received up into glory.

and their own households. **13** For those who have served well as deacons [a]obtain for themselves a [1]high standing and great confidence in the faith that is in Christ Jesus.

1Timothy 3:14 I am writing these things to you, hoping to come to you before long; **15** but [1]in case I am delayed, *I write* so that you will know how [2]one ought to conduct himself in [a]the household of God, which is the [b]church of [c]the living God, the [d]pillar and support of the truth. **16** By common confession, great is [a]the mystery of godliness:

> He who was [b]revealed in the flesh,
> Was [1][c]vindicated [2]in the Spirit,
> [d]Seen by angels,
> [e]Proclaimed among the nations,
> [f]Believed on in the world,
> [g]Taken up in glory.

1Timothy 3:1
[1]Or *bishop*
[a]1 Tim 1:15
[b]Acts 20:28; Phil 1:1

1Timothy 3:2
[1]Lit *The*
[a]1 Tim 3:2-4; Titus 1:6-8
[b]Luke 2:36f; 1 Tim 5:9; Titus 1:6
[c]1 Tim 3:8, 11; Titus 2:2
[d]Rom 12:13; Titus 1:8; Heb 13:2; 1 Pet 4:9
[e]2 Tim 2:24

1Timothy 3:3
[1]Lit *not*
[a]Titus 1:7
[b]1 Tim 3:8; 6:10; Titus 1:7; Heb 13:5

1Timothy 3:4
[a]1 Tim 3:12

1Timothy 3:5
[a]1 Cor 10:32; 1 Tim 3:15

1Timothy 3:6
[1]Lit *of the devil*
[a]1 Tim 6:4; 2 Tim 3:4
[b]1 Tim 3:7

1Timothy 3:7
[a]2 Cor 8:21
[b]Mark 4:11
[c]1 Tim 6:9; 2 Tim 2:26

1Timothy 3:8
[1]Or *given to double-talk*
[2]Lit *not*

[a]Phil 1:1; 1 Tim 3:12
[b]1 Tim 5:23; Titus 2:3
[c]1 Tim 3:3; Titus 1:7; 1 Pet 5:2

1Timothy 3:9
[a]1 Tim 1:5, 19

1Timothy 3:10
[a]1 Tim 5:22

1Timothy 3:11
[1]I.e. either deacons' wives or deaconesses
[a]2 Tim 3:3; Titus 2:3
[b]1 Tim 3:2

1Timothy 3:12
[1]Lit *managing well*
[a]Phil 1:1; 1 Tim 3:8
[b]1 Tim 3:2
[c]1 Tim 3:4

1Timothy 3:13
[1]Lit *good*
[a]Matt 25:21

1Timothy 3:15
[1]Lit *if I delay*
[2]Or *you ought to conduct yourself*
[a]1 Cor 3:16; 2 Cor 6:16; Eph 2:21f; 1 Pet 2:5; 4:17
[b]1 Tim 3:5
[c]Matt 16:16; 1 Tim 4:10
[d]Gal 2:9; 2 Tim 2:19

1Timothy 3:16
[1]Or *justified*
[2]Or *by*
[a]Rom 16:25
[b]John 1:14; 1 Pet 1:20; 1 John 3:5, 8
[c]Rom 3:4
[d]Luke 2:13; 24:4; 1 Pet 1:12
[e]Rom 16:26; 2 Cor 1:19; Col 1:23

f 2 Thess 1:10

g Mark 16:19; Acts 1:9

1Timothy 3:1 Πιστὸς ὁ λόγος· Εἴ τις ἐπισκοπῆς ὀρέγεται, καλοῦ ἔργου ἐπιθυμεῖ. **2** Δεῖ οὖν τὸν ἐπίσκοπον ἀνεπίληπτον εἶναι, μιᾶς γυναικὸς ἄνδρα, νηφάλεον, σώφρονα, κόσμιον, φιλόξενον, διδακτικόν· **3** μὴ πάροινον, μὴ πλήκτην, μὴ αἰσχροκερδῆ, ἀλλ᾽ ἐπιεικῆ, ἄμαχον, ἀφιλάργυρον· **4** τοῦ ἰδίου οἴκου καλῶς προϊστάμενον, τέκνα ἔχοντα ἐν ὑποταγῇ μετὰ πασης σεμνότητος **5** _ Εἴ δέ τις τοῦ ἰδίου οἴκου προστῆναι οὐκ οἶδεν, πῶς ἐκκλησίας θεοῦ ἐπιμελήσεται; **6** Μὴ νεόφυτον, ἵνα μὴ τυφωθεὶς εἰς κρίμα ἐμπέσῃ τοῦ διαβόλου. **7** Δεῖ δὲ αὐτὸν καὶ μαρτυρίαν καλὴν ἔχειν ἀπὸ τῶν ἔξωθεν, ἵνα μὴ εἰς ὀνειδισμὸν ἐμπέσῃ καὶ παγίδα τοῦ διαβόλου. **8** Διακόνους ὡσαύτως σεμνους, μὴ διλόγους, μὴ οἴνῳ πολλῷ προσέχοντας, μὴ αἰσχροκερδεῖς, **9** ἔχοντας τὸ μυστήριον τῆς πίστεως ἐν καθαρᾷ συνειδήσει. **10** Καὶ οὗτοι δὲ δοκιμαζέσθωσαν πρῶτον, εἶτα διακονείτωσαν, ἀνέγκλητοι ὄντες. **11** Γυναῖκας ὡσαύτως σεμνάς, μὴ διαβόλους, νηφαλέους, πιστὰς ἐν πᾶσιν. **12** Διάκονοι ἔστωσαν μιᾶς γυναικὸς ἄνδρες, τέκνων καλῶς προϊστάμενοι καὶ τῶν ἰδίων οἴκων. **13** Οἱ γὰρ καλῶς διακονήσαντες βαθμὸν ἑαυτοῖς καλὸν περιποιοῦνται, καὶ πολλὴν παρρησίαν ἐν πίστει τῇ ἐν χριστῷ Ἰησοῦ.

1Timothy 3:14 Ταῦτά σοι γράφω, ἐλπίζων ἐλθεῖν πρός σε τάχιον· **15** ἐὰν δὲ βραδύνω, ἵνα εἰδῇς πῶς δεῖ ἐν οἴκῳ θεοῦ ἀναστρέφεσθαι, ἥτις ἐστὶν ἐκκλησία θεοῦ ζῶντος, στῦλος καὶ ἑδραίωμα τῆς ἀληθείας. **16** Καὶ ὁμολογουμένως μέγα ἐστὶν τὸ τῆς εὐσεβείας μυστήριον· θεὸς ἐφανερώθη ἐν σαρκί, ἐδικαιώθη ἐν πνεύματι, ὤφθη ἀγγέλοις, ἐκηρύχθη ἐν ἔθνεσιν, ἐπιστεύθη ἐν κόσμῳ, ἀνελήφθη ἐν δόξῃ.

Language

Process of Discovery

Linguistics Section

Linguistic Structure

[Office of Bishop] 1Timothy 3:1 *a*It is a trustworthy statement: if any man aspires to the *b*office of [1]overseer, it is a fine work he desires *to do*. **2** [1a]An overseer, then, must be above reproach, *b*the husband of one wife, *c*temperate, prudent, respectable, *d*hospitable, *e*able to teach, **3** *a*not addicted to wine [1]or pugnacious, but gentle, peaceable, *b*free from the love of money. **4** *He must be* one who *a*manages his own household well, keeping his children under control with all dignity **5** (but if a man does not know how to manage his own household, how will he take care of *a*the church of God?), **6** *and* not a new convert, so that he will not become *a*conceited and fall into the *b*condemnation [1]incurred by the devil. **7** And he must *a*have a good reputation with *b*those outside *the church*, so that he will not fall into reproach and *c*the snare of the devil.

[Office of Deacons] 1Timothy 3:8 *a*Deacons likewise *must be* men of dignity, not [1]double-tongued, [2b]or addicted to much wine [2c]or fond of sordid gain, **9** *a*but holding to the mystery of the faith with a clear conscience. **10** *a*These men must also first be tested; then let them serve as deacons if they are beyond reproach. **11** [1]Women *must* likewise *be* dignified, *a*not malicious gossips, but *b*temperate, faithful in all things. **12** *a*Deacons must be *b*husbands of *only* one wife, *and* [1c]good managers of *their* children and their own households. **13** For those who have served well as deacons *a*obtain for themselves a [1]high standing and great confidence in the faith that is in Christ Jesus.

[Conduct] 1Timothy 3:14 I am writing these things to you, hoping to come to you before long; **15** but [1]in case I am delayed, *I write* so that you will know how [2]one ought to conduct himself in *a*the household of God, which is the *b*church of *c*the living God, the *d*pillar and support of the truth. **16** By common confession, great is *a*the mystery of godliness:

He who was *b*revealed in the flesh,
Was [1c]vindicated [2]in the Spirit,
*d*Seen by angels,
*e*Proclaimed among the nations,
*f*Believed on in the world,
*g*Taken up in glory.

Discussion

The need for overseers, Bishops, is an invention of Paul's.

Questioning the Passage

1. Why did Paul feel it necessary to have bishops (overseers)?

    Today's world synagogues do not have overseers like the church has bishops. Why did Paul want overseers? Simple, the Mithras converted house churches could have easily slipped from being Yeshua worshipers to becoming Mithras worshippers. Also, Paul was extremely concerned that only his form of Christianity survived. His churches were mainly converted Mithras House Churches into Yeshua House Churches. Hierarchy grows and it surely did for the Proto-Orthodox Church. Just look at the leadership structure of the Catholic church. There are numerous layers of management and control between the Pope and the common person in the pews. Paul straddled the church with the burden of hierarchy which has grown tremendously today. Unfortunately, the church in many phases is dying because giving the power of full control to one person will not succeed throughout this century. The supposed checks and balances some denominations occur do not work. For example, in the United Methodist system if the Bishop imposes something that the churches dislike they have to bring the matter to the church courts. By the time the case comes before the court the Bishop is either retired or assigned to another Conference. It is too late to change things. The UMC Bishop selection is unfortunately based on politics and checking boxes. It should be based on leadership skills and creativity. This is another reason the UMC is failing.

2. Why did the Catholic church prevent priests from marriage? (v. 4)?

   Obviously in the early church priests, elders, deacons, and Bishops were allowed to be married. The tradition of celibacy is not biblical. In the Middle Ages during Feudalism, the first-born son inherited his father's property. Land Lords asked the church to create a church for their serfs (their workers). The church would be given some land to grow crops. The local priest was required to send a large portion of the income of the church to Rome. When the priest died the land and building became the property of the first born son. If the son did not want to be controlled by Rome he would cut Rome off. Therefore, Rome lost income. In Feudalism an illegitimate child could not inherit his father's property. Throughout the Middle Ages and early Modernism priests, Bishops and even Popes had illegitimate children. The celibacy rule became a tradition in the Catholic church. The Catholic church judges the world through the lens of tradition, then Bible. It will be difficult to eliminate this requirement.

3. How does the "bishop" control his children? (v. 5)

   The main idea is that a bishop had to ensure that his children stayed in the faith. If the bishop could not control his children to stay as Yeshua followers then what chance did he have with the rest of the congregation. [A personal note: I worked as an Associate Pastor to a Senior Pastor whose children all rejected the faith. The congregation had no confidence in his abilities and moved to have him replaced.]

4. Why is it important to have an excellent reputation outside the church? (v. 7)

   The church has always tried to project itself as a place of grace and love in the community. If the Bishop, elder, or deacon did not have an excellent reputation in town then the town people would not trust that person's leadership and not want to become a part of the congregation.

5. Why is the mystery of the faith? (v. 9)

The mystery of the faith is how atonement works. In the Mithras cult Mithras died for the forgiveness of the sins of his followers. No one really knew how that worked. Paul's conversion of these cult churches was to substitute Yeshua for Mithras. So, how did Yeshua die on the cross offer forgiveness for sins? That is still a mystery today. There are several atonement theologies that have been presented over the centuries. None of them have proof behind them. The Gospels never say that Yeshua died for the forgiveness of sin. That statement is from the Mithras cult. However, if a person emulates Yeshua's words and actions in their lives then they will be following the Torah and Prophets and thus pleasing the LORD. Sin would not enter their lives. Therefore, it can be said that Yeshua's message and mannerisms is what says a person from sin because they will understand how not to sin.

6. Why was it important that the wife be of good nature? (v. 10)

The efficacy of the Bishop, elder or deacon was and is seen in the spouse. Today women can hold these offices therefore this verse can be interpreted as the spouse must be of good nature. If the spouse is anti-church it will be very obvious to the people. They people would question their overseer about this situation. It would be a distraction and an area for gossip to development. Therefore, the attitude and actions of the wife is important to the actions of a bishop. Today substitute "spouse" for "wife"

7. What does it mean to be in a high standing? (v. 13)

To be in high standing means that one has not committed any action that could be viewed as evil or illegal. How can an overseer direct congregations to follow the ways of Yeshua if he cannot do it? Therefore, the bishop had to be someone who had committed any crimes or shading deals.

8. What does the household of God mean? (v. 15)

This is another term for being a member of the Kingdom of God. Paul was not aware of the term "Kingdom of God" or he would have used the term. It is possible that the authors of the Gospels did know this either. Since Paul's letters were written before the first Gospel, Matthew's Gospel, the wording "Kingdom of God" may not have been available. It is therefore possible that Yeshua referred to the "household of God" and not the "Kingdom of God." Since the two are the same it does not matter.

9. What is the truth? (v. 15)

For Paul the truth about Yeshua was what he decided it would be. The church today is built on Paul's letters. Yeshua's words and actions are in the fabric of the church but are only a few standing stones. Paul created the church that we have today. The doctrines of church over the centuries reflect Paul's decisions and its Mithras influence.

10. Why was "forgiveness of sin" missing in verse sixteen?

The mystery of why some people seem to have been given an extra dose of grace is blocked from us. Why did the LORD choose Abraham or Moses? This is a question that Yeshua never addressed. Paul offered a list. Perhaps the forgiveness of sin was omitted because it was an automatic thing for Paul. When a person was baptized into the faith they automatically received the forgiveness of sin from Yeshua. Therefore, he probably did not feel it was necessary to repeat the obvious.

11. What does "seen by angels" mean? (v. 16)

The concept of being "seen by an angel" can have different interpretations and meanings, depending on one's religious or spiritual beliefs. In various religious traditions, angels are often considered to be messengers or beings with a divine connection, and their interactions with humans are significant.

Protection and Guidance: In many religious texts and beliefs, angels are seen as beings sent by a higher power to protect, guide, and assist individuals in times of need. Being seen by an angel could symbolize divine protection or guidance during a difficult or challenging situation.

Divine Intervention: Some people believe that being seen by an angel implies that a divine presence is watching over them and intervening in their life. This could be a comforting or reassuring thought during times of hardship or uncertainty.

Spiritual Awakening: Being seen by an angel may also be interpreted as a sign of a spiritual awakening or a heightened awareness of one's connection to the spiritual or divine realm. It could represent a moment of enlightenment or insight.

Messages from the Divine: Angels are often viewed as messengers of the divine. If one feels they have been seen by an angel, it might be seen as a sign that a message or insight is being conveyed to them, either through a dream, intuition, or a meaningful encounter.

Symbolism and Allegory: In literature and art, being seen by an angel can be a symbolic or allegorical representation of being recognized for one's virtues, purity, or righteousness. It may symbolize being acknowledged for one's good deeds or moral character.

It's important to note that beliefs about angels and their interactions with humans vary widely among different cultures and religious traditions. For some, angelic encounters are deeply personal and spiritual experiences, while for others, they may be viewed more symbolically or metaphorically. The interpretation of being seen by an angel ultimately depends on an individual's beliefs and experiences.

12. What does "justified in the Spirit" mean? (v. 16)

The phrase "justified in the Spirit" is a theological concept that is often associated with Christian beliefs, particularly in the context of Christian salvation and righteousness. It comes from the New Testament of the Bible, specifically from passages in the writings of the Apostle Paul, who played a significant role in shaping Christian theology. Here is an explanation of what "justified in the Spirit" means within this Christian context:

Justification: In Christian theology, justification refers to the act of God declaring a sinner to be righteous or just in His sight. It is the forgiveness of sins and the declaration that a person is in right standing with God. This concept is fundamental to the Christian understanding of salvation.

The phrase "in the Spirit" often refers to the work of the Holy Spirit, who Christians believe plays a central role in the process of salvation and sanctification in Christian theology. Being "in the Spirit" means being under the influence and guidance of the Holy Spirit.

When someone is said to be "justified in the Spirit," it means that the work of the Holy Spirit within them is the basis for their righteousness and acceptance before God, rather than their own efforts or works. In Christian theology, it is believed that the Holy Spirit works in the life of a believer, convicting them of sin, leading them to repentance, and empowering them to live a life under God's will.

The belief underscores that salvation and righteousness are not earned through human efforts but that God's grace and the work of the Holy Spirit grant them, emphasizing the idea of being "justified in the Spirit." It emphasizes the importance of faith and trust in God's mercy and forgiveness as the means by which individuals are declared righteous in His sight. This concept is a central aspect of Christian soteriology, which is the study of the doctrine of salvation.

Discussion

There were high penalties for people to pay if they changed their religion. Punishments were the cutting off of hands, legs, and other members of the body. There was no mercy and forgiveness for joining the faith in Yeshua. The pagan priests would try to capture the convert and perform a penalty n them. Paul admonished this practice and required the elders and priests to be meek, and loving. If a person left the congregation, there was to be no retaliation. The church would also protect a convert from their pagan priest.

Thoughts

Paul was so concerned that his churches would survive that he created a hierarchy which the church of today is saddled with. Independent churches are thriving today because they do not have to pay for the hierarchy, and they do not have to take orders from the "ivory tower." The Bishop of a territory rarely understands that the northern parts of the territory might think differently than the southern parts do.

Therefore, the Bishops come up with rules that a part of their territory will love and another will hate. The bishops and above are the highest paid clergy in the church. For centuries political maneuverings gained the office of Archbishop and above. This method allows unqualified people to step into leadership and the result is the 1,000+ denominations.

Chapter Four

Language

Peshitta	New American Standard 1995
1Tim. 4:1 But the Spirit saith explicitly, that in the latter times, some will depart from the faith; and will go after deceptive spirits, and after the doctrine of demons. [2] These will seduce, by a false appearance; and will utter a lie, and will be seared in their conscience; [3] and will forbid to marry; and will require abstinence from meats, which God hath created for use and for thankfulness, by them who believe and know the truth. [4] Because whatever is created by God is good; and there is nothing which should be rejected if it be received with thankfulness; [5] for it is sanctified by the word of God and by prayer. [6] If thou shalt inculcate these things on thy brethren, thou wilt be a good minister of Jesus the Messiah, being educated in the language of the faith, and in the good doctrine which thou hast been taught. [7] But the silly tales of old women, shun thou; and occupy thyself with righteousness. [8] For, exercising the body is profitable a little while; but righteousness is every way profitable and hath promise of the life of the present time and of that to come. [9] This is a faithful saying, and worthy of reception. [10] For on this account, we toil and suffer reproach; because we trust in the living God, who is the life-giver of all men, especially of the believers. [11] These things teach thou, and inculcate. [12] And let no one despise thy youth; but be thou a pattern for the	**1Tim. 4:1** But [a]the Spirit explicitly says that [b]in later times some will [1]fall away from the faith, paying attention to [c]deceitful spirits and [d]doctrines of demons, [2] by means of the hypocrisy of liars [a]seared in their own conscience as with a branding iron, [3] *men* who [a]forbid marriage *and advocate* [b]abstaining from foods which [c]God has created to be [d]gratefully shared in by those who believe and know the truth. [4] For [a]everything created by God is good, and nothing is to be rejected if it is [b]received with gratitude; [5] for it is sanctified by means of [a]the word of God and prayer. *A Good Minister's Discipline* **1Tim. 4:6** In pointing out these things to [a]the brethren, you will be a good [b]servant of Christ Jesus, *constantly* nourished on the words of the faith and of the [1c]sound doctrine which you [d]have been following. [7] But [1]have nothing to do with [a]worldly [b]fables fit only for old women. On the other hand, discipline yourself for the purpose of [c]godliness; [8] for [a]bodily discipline is only of little profit, but [b]godliness is profitable for all things, since it [c]holds promise for the [d]present life and *also* for the *life* to come. [9] [a]It is a trustworthy statement deserving full acceptance. [10] For it is for this we labor and strive, because we have fixed [a]our hope on

believers, in speech, and in behavior, and in love, and in faith, and in purity. ¹³ Until I come, be diligent in reading, and in prayer, and in teaching. ¹⁴ Despise not the gift that is in thee, which was given thee by prophecy, and by the laying on of the hand of the eldership. ¹⁵ On these things meditate; give thyself wholly to them: that it may be obvious to all that thou makest advances. ¹⁶ Be attentive to thyself, and to thy teaching; and persevere in them. For in doing this, thou wilt procure life to thyself and to them who hear thee.

*b*the living God, who is *c*the Savior of all men, especially of believers.

1Tim. 4:11 ¹¹*a*Prescribe and teach these things. ¹² *a*Let no one look down on your youthfulness, but *rather* in speech, conduct, *b*love, faith *and* purity, show yourself *c*an example ¹of those who believe. ¹³ *a*Until I come, give attention to the *public* *b*reading *of Scripture*, to exhortation and teaching. ¹⁴ Do not neglect the spiritual gift within you, which was bestowed on you through *a*prophetic utterance with *b*the laying on of hands by the ¹*c*presbytery. ¹⁵ Take pains with these things; be *absorbed* in them, so that your progress will be evident to all. ¹⁶ *a*Pay close attention to yourself and to your teaching; persevere in these things, for as you do this you will ¹*b*ensure salvation both for yourself and for those who hear you.

1Timothy 4:1
[1]I.e. apostacize
[a]John 16:13; Acts 20:23; 21:11; 1 Cor 2:10f
[b]2 Thess 2:3ff; 2 Tim 3:1; 2 Pet 3:3; Jude 18
[c]1 John 4:6
[d]James 3:15

1Timothy 4:2
[a]Eph 4:19

1Timothy 4:3
[a]Heb 13:4
[b]Col 2:16, 23
[c]Gen 1:29; 9:3
[d]Rom 14:6; 1 Cor 10:30f; 1 Tim 4:4

1Timothy 4:4
[a]1 Cor 10:26
[b]Rom 14:6; 1 Cor 10:30f; 1 Tim 4:3

1Timothy 4:5
[a]Gen 1:25, 31; Heb 11:3

1Timothy 4:6
[1]Lit *good*
[a]Acts 1:15
[b]2 Cor 11:23
[c]1 Tim 1:10
[d]Luke 1:3; Phil 2:20, 22; 2 Tim 3:10

1Timothy 4:7
[1]Or *reject*
[a]1 Tim 1:9
[b]1 Tim 1:4
[c]1 Tim 4:8; 6:3, 5f; 2 Tim 3:5

1Timothy 4:8
[a]Col 2:23

[b]1 Tim 4:7; 6:3, 5f; 2 Tim 3:5
[c]Ps 37:9, 11; Prov 19:23; 22:4; Matt 6:33
[d]Matt 6:33; 12:32; Mark 10:30

1Timothy 4:9
[a]1 Tim 1:15

1Timothy 4:10
[a]2 Cor 1:10; 1 Tim 6:17
[b]1 Tim 3:15
[c]John 4:42; 1 Tim 2:4

1Timothy 4:11
[1]Or *Keep commanding and teaching*
[a]1 Tim 5:7; 6:2

1Timothy 4:12
[1]Or *to*
[a]1 Cor 16:11; Titus 2:15
[b]Titus 2:7; 1 Pet 5:3
[c]1 Tim 1:14

1Timothy 4:13
[a]1 Tim 3:14
[b]2 Tim 3:15ff

1Timothy 4:14
[1]Or *board of elders*
[a]1 Tim 1:18
[b]Acts 6:6; 1 Tim 5:22; 2 Tim 1:6
[c]Acts 11:30

1Timothy 4:16
[1]Lit *save both yourself and those*
[a]Acts 20:28
[b]1 Cor 1:21

Koine Greek

1Tim. 4:1 Το δε πνευμα ρητως λεγει οτι εν υστεροις καιροις αποστησονται τινες της πιστεως προσεχοντες πνευμασιν πλανοις και διδασκαλιαις δαιμονιων, ² εν υποκρισει ψευδολογων, κεκαυστηριασμενων την ιδιαν συνειδησιν, ³ κωλυοντων γαμειν, απεχεσθαι βρωματων, α ο θεος εκτισεν εις μεταλημψιν μετα ευχαριστιας τοις πιστοις και επεγνωκοσι την αληθειαν. ⁴ οτι παν κτισμα θεου καλον και ουδεν αποβλητον μετα ευχαριστιας λαμβανομενον· ⁵ αγιαζεται γαρ δια λογου θεου και εντευξεως.

1Tim. 4:6 Ταυτα υποτιθεμενος τοις αδελφοις καλος εση διακονος Χριστου Ιησου, εντρεφομενος τοις λογοις της πιστεως και της καλης διδασκαλιας η παρηκολουθηκας· ⁷ τους δε βεβηλους και γραωδεις μυθους παραιτου. Γυμναζε δε σεαυτον προς ευσεβειαν· ⁸ η γαρ σωματικη γυμνασια προς ολιγον εστιν ωφελιμος, η δε ευσεβεια προς παντα ωφελιμος εστιν επαγγελιαν εχουσα ζωης της νυν και της μελλουσης. ⁹ πιστος ο λογος και πασης αποδοχης αξιος· ¹⁰ εις τουτο γαρ κοπιωμεν και αγωνιζομεθα, οτι ηλπικαμεν επι θεω ζωντι, ος εστιν σωτηρ παντων ανθρωπων μαλιστα πιστων.

1Tim. 4:11 Παραγγελλε ταυτα και διδασκε. ¹² Μηδεις σου της νεοτητος καταφρονειτω, αλλα τυπος γινου των πιστων εν λογω, εν αναστροφη, εν αγαπη, εν πιστει, εν αγνεια. ¹³ εως ερχομαι προσεχε τη αναγνωσει, τη παρακλησει, τη διδασκαλια. ¹⁴ μη αμελει του εν σοι χαρισματος, ο εδοθη σοι δια προφητειας μετα επιθεσεως των χειρων του πρεσβυτεριου. ¹⁵ ταυτα μελετα, εν τουτοις ισθι, ινα σου η προκοπη φανερα η πασιν. ¹⁶ επεχε σεαυτω και τη διδασκαλια, επιμενε αυτοις· τουτο γαρ ποιων και σεαυτον σωσεις και τους ακουοντας σου.

Language

Process of Discovery

Linguistics Section

Linguistic Structure

Discussion

1. What is the doctrine of demons? (v. 1)

   The doctrine of demons refers to teachings that were false and could lead people to be misled. Paul believed that his expression of Christianity was the only legitimate one. He was always concerned that his converted Mithras churches would return to Mithras worship. He also was not a fan of the Gnostics and other Christian expressions that started to rise during his lifetime. He constantly warned all of his converted churches about these other groups.

2. What does it mean that the Spirit explicitly says? (v. 1)

   The usage of the word "Spirits" in this chapter means "prophecies." When men or women prophesy, they would say that they were moved by the Spirit of God.

3. What does it mean to be seared in their own conscience as with a branding iron? (v. 2)

   A branding iron when heated and placed on the skin will leave a scare. This practice is done today to identify ownership of farm animals. This expression means that a view or opinion will become a permanent fixture of ones mind.

4. Why does Paul imply that marriage is fine? (v. 3)

   There were groups of Yeshua's followers who were not a part of Paul's movement who was celibacy as acceptable. The Essences and Sabians had such doctrines. Paul viewed their views as unacceptable to the new Christian churches. Marriage was also discouraged by these groups and at times denounced it as evil. Men would damage their reproductive organs denouncing evil in hopes that they would get into the Kingdom of God easily and quickly. Paul denounced these acts in this letter. If marriage was removed then the group would die out unless they brought in new followers. This verse seems to contradict Paul's view of marriage. In other letters Paul said that it was not wise to marry because he believed that Yeshua would return in his lifetime. However, he never condemned it. He believed that it was not prudent and would detract from the believers worship to Yeshua.

5. What foods to abstain from (Kosher or sacrificed to idols)? (v. 3)
This is possibly a reference to Kosher foods. There was a large number of Christian-Jews who traveled from Jerusalem to Asia Minor inorder to convince people in Paul's converted churches that if they wanted to follow the Jewish Messiah that they had to become prostelytes first. That would entail eating Kosher food and disposing of all of their false gods and idols.

6. What does it mean to receive with gratitude? (v. 4)
How many times have people today felt that they produced their wealth and prosperity and that God had nothing to do with it? To receive with gratitude is to be thankful to the LORD for everything one has.

7. What does verse five mean?
To be sanctified by the Word of God means that whatever it is you are thinking or doing is mentioned as good in the Scripture.

8. What does it mean to be nourished on the words of faith and sound doctrine? (v. 6)

The nourishment has to do with the building and supporting of one's faith. When Paul refers to sound doctrine he is referring to his definition of Christianity. The Proto-Orthodox church which evolved into the churches of today are based on Paul's doctrine about what Yeshua's life and death means. The earliest expression of the Proto-Orthodox church was based on Mithras. Paul accepted Mithras doctrine which explains how the Messiah's death cleansed the followers of their sins.

9. What are the silly tales of old women? (v. 7)

Near Eastern women, especially the elderly, loved to tell stories. Many times the stories were elaborated so much over the years that the original story was lost. "I cannot believe it; it is a saying of an old woman" was a phrase used to describe these stories,.

10. What is bodily disciples? (v. 8)

Bodily disciple is taking good care of one's body. Exercise and staying at a proper weight are examples of bodily disciples.

11. What is godliness? (v. 8)

This is the practice of God's laws which are contained in the Bible.

12. What does verse ten mean (why God and not Christ who saves)? (v. 10)

It is interesting that in this verse the author refers to God as the Savior and not to Christ. It is not clear why the author used this language. The church interpretation is that the author is telling us that Christ is God. Therefore, God

Chapter Five

Language

Peshitta	New American Standard 1995
1Tim. 5:1 Chide not an elder, but entreat him as a father; and the younger men, as thy brothers; ² and the elder women, as mothers; and the younger women, as thy sisters, with all purity. ³ Honor widows, who are truly widows. ⁴ But if a widow hath children, or grandchildren, let them first learn to show kindness to their own households, and to repay the obligations to their parents; for this is acceptable before God. ⁵ Now she who is truly a widow, and solitary, her hope is in God; and she persevereth in prayers, and in supplications, by night and by day: ⁶ But she who followeth pleasure, is dead while she liveth. ⁷ These things enjoin thou on them, that they may be blameless. ⁸ But if any one careth not for them who are his own, and especially for them who are of the household of faith, he hath rejected the faith, and is worse than the unbelievers. ⁹ Therefore elect thou the widow, who is not less than sixty years [old], and who hath been the wife of one man, ¹⁰ and hath a reputation for good works; if she have trained up children, if she have entertained strangers, if she have washed the feet of saints, if she have relieved the afflicted, if she have walked in every good work. ¹¹ But the younger widows do thou reject; for they wax wanton against the Messiah, and desire to be married: ¹² and their condemnation is fixed, because they have cast off their former faith. ¹³ And they also learn idleness, wandering from house to house; and not only idleness, but also to talk much, and to pursue vanities, and to utter what they ought not. ¹⁴ I would therefore, that the younger women marry, and bear children, and regulate their houses; and that they give no occasion to	**1Tim. 5:1** ᵃDo not sharply rebuke an ᵇolder man, but *rather* appeal to *him* as a father, *to* ᶜthe younger men as brothers, ² the older women as mothers, *and* the younger women as sisters, in all purity. **1Tim. 5:3** Honor widows who are ᵃwidows indeed; ⁴ but if any widow has children or grandchildren, ᵃthey must first learn to practice piety in regard to their own family and to ¹make some return to their parents; for this is ᵇacceptable in the sight of God. ⁵ Now she who is a ᵃwidow indeed and who has been left alone, ᵇhas fixed her hope on God and continues in ᶜentreaties and prayers night and day. ⁶ But she who ᵃgives herself to wanton pleasure is ᵇdead even while she lives. ⁷ ¹ᵃPrescribe these things as well, so that they may be above reproach. ⁸ But if anyone does not provide for his own, and especially for those of his household, he has ᵃdenied the faith and is worse than an unbeliever. **1Tim. 5:9** A widow is to be ᵃput on the list only if she is not less than sixty years old, *having been* ᵇthe wife of one man, ¹⁰ having a reputation for ᵃgood works; *and* if she has brought up children, if she has ᵇshown hospitality to strangers, if she ᶜhas washed the ¹saints' feet, if she has ᵈassisted those in distress, *and* if she has devoted herself to every good work. ¹¹ But refuse *to put* younger widows *on the list,* for when they feel ᵃsensual desires in disregard of Christ, they want to get married, ¹² *thus* incurring condemnation, because they have set aside their previous

the adversary for reproach. ¹⁵ For some have already begun to turn aside after Satan. ¹⁶ If any believing man or believing woman have widows, let them support them; and let them not be a burden on the church; so that there may be a sufficiency for such as are really widows. ¹⁷ Let the elders who conduct themselves well, be esteemed worthy of double honor; especially they who labor in the word and in doctrine. ¹⁸ For the scripture saith Thou shalt not muzzle the ox in threshing; and, The laborer is worthy of his pay. ¹⁹ Against an elder, receive not a complaint, except at the mouth of two or three witnesses. ²⁰ Those who sin before all rebuke; that the rest of the people may fear. ²¹ I charge thee, before God, and our Lord Jesus the Messiah, and his elect angels, that thou observe these things; and let not your mind be preoccupied by any thing: and do nothing with a respect for persons. ²² Lay not the hand hastily on any man; and participate not in the sins of others; keep thyself pure. ²³ And hereafter drink not water, but drink a little wine; on account of thy stomach, and thy continuing infirmities. ²⁴ There are persons, whose sins are known, and go before them to the place of judgment; and there are some, whom they follow after. ²⁵ So also good deeds are known: and those which are otherwise cannot be hid.

¹pledge. ¹³ At the same time they also learn *to be* idle, as they go around from house to house; and not merely idle, but also ᵃgossips and ᵇbusybodies, talking about ᶜthings not proper *to mention.* ¹⁴ Therefore, I want younger *widows* to get ᵃmarried, bear children, ᵇkeep house, *and* ᶜgive the enemy no occasion for reproach; ¹⁵ for some ᵃhave already turned aside to follow ᵇSatan. ¹⁶ If any woman who is a believer ᵃhas *dependent* widows, she must ᵇassist them and the church must not be burdened, so that it may assist those who are ᶜwidows indeed.

Concerning Elders

1Tim. 5:17 ᵃThe elders who ᵇrule well are to be considered worthy of double honor, especially those who ᶜwork hard ¹at preaching and teaching. ¹⁸ For the Scripture says, "ᵃYOU SHALL NOT MUZZLE THE OX WHILE HE IS THRESHING," and "ᵇThe laborer is worthy of his wages." ¹⁹ Do not receive an accusation against an ᵃelder except on the basis of ᵇtwo or three witnesses. ²⁰ Those who continue in sin, ᵃrebuke in the presence of all, ᵇso that the rest also will be fearful *of sinning.* ²¹ ᵃI solemnly charge you in the presence of God and of Christ Jesus and of *His* chosen angels, to maintain these *principles* without bias, doing nothing in a *spirit of* partiality. ²² ᵃDo not lay hands upon anyone *too* hastily and ¹thereby share ᵇresponsibility *for* the sins of others; keep yourself ²free from sin.

1Tim. 5:23 No longer drink water *exclusively,* but ᵃuse a little wine for the sake of your stomach and your frequent ailments.

1Tim. 5:24 The sins of some men are quite evident, going before them to judgment; for others, their *sins* ᵃfollow after. ²⁵ Likewise also,

	deeds that are good are quite evident, and ᵃthose which are otherwise cannot be concealed.

1Timothy 5:1
[a]Lev 19:32
[b]Titus 2:2
[c]Titus 2:6

1Timothy 5:3
[a]Acts 6:1; 9:39, 41; 1 Tim 5:5, 16

1Timothy 5:4
[1]Lit *give back recompenses*
[a]Eph 6:2
[b]1 Tim 2:3

1Timothy 5:5
[a]Acts 6:1; 9:39, 41; 1 Tim 5:3, 16
[b]1 Cor 7:34; 1 Pet 3:5
[c]Luke 2:37; 1 Tim 2:1; 2 Tim 1:3

1Timothy 5:6
[a]James 5:5
[b]Luke 15:24; 2 Tim 3:6; Rev 3:1

1Timothy 5:7
[1]Or *Keep commanding*
[a]1 Tim 4:11

1Timothy 5:8
[a]2 Tim 2:12; Titus 1:16; 2 Pet 2:1; Jude 4

1Timothy 5:9
[a]1 Tim 5:16
[b]1 Tim 3:2

1Timothy 5:10
[1]Or *holy ones*
[a]Acts 9:36; 1 Tim 6:18; Titus 2:7; 3:8; 1 Pet 2:12
[b]1 Tim 3:2

*c*Luke 7:44; John 13:14
*d*1 Tim 5:16

1Timothy 5:11
*a*Rev 18:7

1Timothy 5:12
[1]Lit *faith*

1Timothy 5:13
*a*3 John 10
*b*2 Thess 3:11
*c*Titus 1:11

1Timothy 5:14
*a*1 Cor 7:9; 1 Tim 4:3
*b*Titus 2:5
*c*1 Tim 6:1

1Timothy 5:15
*a*1 Tim 1:20
*b*Matt 4:10

1Timothy 5:16
*a*1 Tim 5:4
*b*1 Tim 5:10
*c*1 Tim 5:3

1Timothy 5:17
[1]Lit *in word*
*a*Acts 11:30; 1 Tim 4:14; 5:19
*b*Rom 12:8
*c*1 Thess 5:12

1Timothy 5:18
*a*Deut 25:4; 1 Cor 9:9
*b*Lev 19:13; Deut 24:15; Matt 10:10; Luke 10:7; 1 Cor 9:14

1Timothy 5:19
*a*Acts 11:30; 1 Tim 4:14; 5:17
*b*Deut 17:6; 19:15; Matt 18:16

1Timothy 5:20
[a]Gal 2:14; Eph 5:11; 2 Tim 4:2
[b]2 Cor 7:11

1Timothy 5:21
[a]Luke 9:26; 1 Tim 6:13; 2 Tim 2:14; 4:1

1Timothy 5:22
[1]Lit *do not share*
[2]Lit *pure*
[a]1 Tim 3:10; 4:14
[b]Eph 5:11; 1 Tim 3:2-7

1Timothy 5:23
[a]1 Tim 3:8

1Timothy 5:24
[a]Rev 14:13

1Timothy 5:25
[a]Prov 10:9

Koine Greek

1Timothy 5:1 Πρεσβυτέρῳ μὴ ἐπιπλήξῃς, ἀλλὰ παρακάλει ὡς πατέρα· νεωτέρους, ὡς ἀδελφούς· 2 πρεσβυτέρας, ὡς μητέρας· νεωτέρας, ὡς ἀδελφάς, ἐν πάσῃ ἁγνείᾳ. 3 Χήρας τίμα τὰς ὄντως χήρας. 4 Εἰ δέ τις χήρα τέκνα ἢ ἔκγονα ἔχει, μανθανέτωσαν πρῶτον τὸν ἴδιον οἶκον εὐσεβεῖν, καὶ ἀμοιβὰς ἀποδιδόναι τοῖς προγόνοις· τοῦτο γάρ ἐστιν ἀπόδεκτον ἐνώπιον τοῦ θεοῦ. 5 Ἡ δὲ ὄντως χήρα καὶ μεμονωμένη ἤλπικεν ἐπὶ τὸν θεόν, καὶ προσμένει ταῖς δεήσεσιν καὶ ταῖς προσευχαῖς νυκτὸς καὶ ἡμέρας. 6 Ἡ δὲ σπαταλῶσα, ζῶσα τέθνηκεν. 7 Καὶ ταῦτα παράγγελλε, ἵνα ἀνεπίληπτοι ὦσιν. 8 Εἰ δέ τις τῶν ἰδίων καὶ μάλιστα τῶν οἰκείων οὐ προνοεῖ, τὴν πίστιν ἤρνηται, καὶ ἔστιν ἀπίστου χείρων. 9 Χήρα καταλεγέσθω μὴ ἔλαττον ἐτῶν ἐξήκοντα, γεγονυῖα ἑνὸς ἀνδρὸς γυνή, 10 ἐν ἔργοις καλοῖς μαρτυρουμένη, εἰ ἐτεκνοτρόφησεν, εἰ ἐξενοδόχησεν, εἰ ἁγίων πόδας ἔνιψεν, εἰ θλιβομένοις ἐπήρκεσεν, εἰ παντὶ ἔργῳ ἀγαθῷ ἐπηκολούθησεν. 11 Νεωτέρας δὲ χήρας παραιτοῦ· ὅταν γὰρ καταστρηνιάσωσιν τοῦ χριστοῦ, γαμεῖν θέλουσιν, 12 ἔχουσαι κρίμα, ὅτι τὴν πρώτην πίστιν ἠθέτησαν. 13 Ἅμα δὲ καὶ ἀργαὶ μανθάνουσιν, περιερχόμεναι τὰς οἰκίας, οὐ μόνον δὲ ἀργαί, ἀλλὰ καὶ φλύαροι καὶ περίεργοι, λαλοῦσαι τὰ μὴ δέοντα. 14 Βούλομαι οὖν νεωτέρας γαμεῖν, τεκνογονεῖν, οἰκοδεσποτεῖν, μηδεμίαν ἀφορμὴν διδόναι τῷ ἀντικειμένῳ λοιδορίας χάριν. 15 Ἤδη γὰρ τινες ἐξετράπησαν ὀπίσω τοῦ Σατανᾶ. 16 Εἴ τις πιστὸς ἢ πιστὴ ἔχει χήρας, ἐπαρκείτω αὐταῖς, καὶ μὴ βαρείσθω ἡ ἐκκλησία, ἵνα ταῖς ὄντως χήραις ἐπαρκέσῃ.

1Timothy 5:17 Οἱ καλῶς προεστῶτες πρεσβύτεροι διπλῆς τιμῆς ἀξιούσθωσαν, μάλιστα οἱ κοπιῶντες ἐν λόγῳ καὶ διδασκαλίᾳ. 18 Λέγει γὰρ ἡ γραφή, Βοῦν ἀλοῶντα οὐ φιμώσεις. καί, Ἄξιος ὁ ἐργάτης τοῦ μισθοῦ αὐτοῦ. 19 Κατὰ πρεσβυτέρου κατηγορίαν μὴ παραδέχου, ἐκτὸς εἰ μὴ ἐπὶ δύο ἢ τριῶν μαρτύρων. 20 Τοὺς ἁμαρτάνοντας ἐνώπιον πάντων ἔλεγχε, ἵνα καὶ οἱ λοιποὶ φόβον ἔχωσιν. 21 Διαμαρτύρομαι ἐνώπιον τοῦ θεοῦ καὶ κυρίου Ἰησοῦ χριστοῦ καὶ τῶν ἐκλεκτῶν ἀγγέλων, ἵνα ταῦτα φυλάξῃς χωρὶς προκρίματος, μηδὲν ποιῶν κατὰ πρόσκλησιν. 22 Χεῖρας ταχέως μηδενὶ ἐπιτίθει, μηδὲ κοινώνει ἁμαρτίαις ἀλλοτρίαις· σεαυτὸν ἁγνὸν τήρει. 23 Μηκέτι ὑδροπότει, ἀλλ᾽ οἴνῳ ὀλίγῳ χρῶ, διὰ τὸν στόμαχόν σου καὶ τὰς πυκνάς σου ἀσθενείας. 24 Τινῶν ἀνθρώπων αἱ ἁμαρτίαι πρόδηλοί εἰσιν, προάγουσαι εἰς κρίσιν· τισὶν δὲ καὶ ἐπακολουθοῦσιν. 25 Ὡσαύτως καὶ τὰ καλὰ ἔργα πρόδηλα ἐστιν· καὶ τὰ ἄλλως ἔχοντα κρυβῆναι οὐ δύνανται.

Language
  Process of Discovery

  Linguistics Section

  Linguistic Structure

[Older men] 1Tim. 5:1 *a*Do not sharply rebuke an *b*older man, but *rather* appeal to *him* as a father, *to* *c*the younger men as brothers, **2** the older women as mothers, *and* the younger women as sisters, in all purity.

[Widows] 1Tim. 5:3 Honor widows who are *a*widows indeed; **4** but if any widow has children or grandchildren, *a*they must first learn to practice piety in regard to their own family and to *1*make some return to their parents; for this is *b*acceptable in the sight of God. **5** Now she who is a *a*widow indeed and who has been left alone, *b*has fixed her hope on God and continues in *c*entreaties and prayers night and day. **6** But she who *a*gives herself to wanton pleasure is *b*dead even while she lives. **7** *1a*Prescribe these things as well, so that they may be above reproach. **8** But if anyone does not provide for his own, and especially for those of his household, he has *a*denied the faith and is worse than an unbeliever. *9*A widow is to be *a*put on the list only if she is not less than sixty years old, *having been* *b*the wife of one man, **10** having a reputation for *a*good works; *and* if she has brought up children, if she has *b*shown hospitality to strangers, if she *c*has washed the *1*saints' feet, if she has *d*assisted those in distress, *and* if she has devoted herself to every good work. **11** But refuse *to put* younger widows *on the list,* for when they feel *a*sensual desires in disregard of Christ, they want to get married, **12** *thus* incurring condemnation, because they have set aside their previous *1*pledge. **13** At the same time they also learn *to be* idle, as they go around from house to house; and not merely idle, but also *a*gossips and *b*busybodies, talking about *c*things not proper *to mention.* **14** Therefore, I want younger *widows* to get *a*married, bear children, *b*keep house, *and* *c*give the enemy no occasion for reproach; **15** for some *a*have already turned aside to follow *b*Satan. **16** If any woman who is a believer *a*has *dependent* widows, she must *b*assist them and the church must not be burdened, so that it may assist those who are *c*widows indeed.

[Elders as Judges] 1Tim. 5:17 *a*The elders who *b*rule well are to be considered worthy of double honor, especially those who *c*work hard *1*at preaching and teaching. **18** For the Scripture says, "*a*YOU SHALL NOT MUZZLE THE OX WHILE HE IS THRESHING," and "*b*The laborer is worthy of his wages." **19** Do not receive an accusation against an *a*elder except on the basis of *b*two or three witnesses. **20** Those who continue in sin, *a*rebuke in the presence of all, *b*so that the rest also will be fearful *of* *sinning.* **21** *ª*I solemnly charge you in the presence of God and of Christ Jesus and of *His* chosen angels, to maintain these *principles* without bias, doing nothing in a *spirit of partiality.* **22** *ª*Do not lay hands upon anyone *too* hastily and ¹thereby share *ᵇresponsibility for* the sins of others; keep yourself ²free from sin.

[Exhortations] 1Tim. 5:23 No longer drink water *exclusively,* but *ª*use a little wine for the sake of your stomach and your frequent ailments. **1Tim. 5:24** The sins of some men are quite evident, going before them to judgment; for others, their *sins ª*follow after. **25** Likewise also, deeds that are good are quite evident, and *ª*those which are otherwise cannot be concealed.

Discussion

This chapter defines who was a widow who deserved church assistance. This seems contradictory to the ideals of Christianity. People in need are generally assisted by the church. The difficultly then and today is that the church is limited in how much help it can give out.

Questioning the Passage

1. Why is their a distinction about "real" widows? (v. 3 & 5)

   The verses read that there is a difference between widows and real widows. There was no doubt what a widow was. As today a married woman whose husband dies is a widow. The term "real widow" is used to determine whether the widow should be supported by the church. The verses three to nine define which widows can receive church help.

2. What are the obligations in verse four?

   Widows were asked to seek help from their family first. The children should take in their widowed mother. The obligation is the time and money spent on raising the children. This is a way to repay that obligation. When a woman became a widow she would have to rely on either the family, the church, or become a prostitute in order to survive. Jewish law is explicit that widowed mothers were to be taken care of by the children. Since this is mentioned in the letter it can be assumed that this was not the practice of some of the Mithras House churches. Since these converted churches kept their old practices Paul wanted to instill a new way of dealing with widowed family members.

3. What are the widows supposed to know? (v. 6 & 7)

A godly woman is one who tries to do everything that she can for the LORD. Some widows advanced their civil life enjoying the pleasures of the Roman culture which are contrary to Christian ideals of that day.

4. Why is the author saying that not taking care of one's family is a denying of the faith? (v. 8)

This is a Christian doctrine that the author decided to explain. It is not biblical nor something Yeshua said. Truly one should be willing to take care of his or her nuclear family. Today there is the question of how far from the nucleus is one expected to help. In ancient days the extended family would be living next to each other. Everything the family did was done for the togetherness of the family. The Christian converts moved into communes. In the communes they attended to each other's needs. Therefore if a person neglected his or her own family it was assumed that the person could not take care of anyone in the community.

5. What does "the wife of one man?" (v. 9)

It was unusual for a widow to remarry. Leviticus says that twice a widow is not permitted to remarry. The reason for this is found in the Zohar. It was believed that a twice widow had found her soul mate in the first husband and the LORD would allow a second marriage. A purpose of marriage was to find a soul mate, even though marriages were prearranged.

6. Why the age of sixty in verse nine?

It was the custom of the time.

7. Why would a widow be alienated from Christ by remarrying? (v. 11)

The verse is referring to young women. Widows who needed support form the church would do tasks for the church. The author believed that the young widows might be looking to find a husband and if they did the work they performed would not be completed.

8. How does remarriage violate the previous marriage pledge? (v. 12)

If the widow married a man who was not a Christian then culture dictated that the widow follow the religion of the husband. Therefore, young widows might not stay in the church as older ones would.

9. Why does one need two or three witnesses? (v. 19)

Two or three witnesses are required when brining forth a complaint or a situation that a judge would need to resolve. This comes from Deut 17:6, 19:15, and Matt 18:16

10. Why does one have to share the responsibility for the sins of others? (v. 22)

It was believed that laying hands upon a sinner could transfer the sin to the person doing the laying of hands. Therefore, the author offers a strong warning against it.

11. Why were the people only drinking water? (v. 23)

The author is saying that wine was used like medicine for some illnesses and discomforts. The author is not supporting the usage of wine. Perhaps this congregation did not know about the medicinal purpose of wine.

12. What are the sins that follow a person to judgment that cannot be seen? (v. 25)

The author is referring to sins that a person is not accountable for because no one knows that he or she committed the sin.

Culture Section

Discussion

Near Eastern women usually married only once in their lifetime. Divorces were rare and difficult to obtain. If a widow remarried and that husband died it became the obligation of the stepchildren to attend to her needs. Women over sixty years old who decided not to remarry and had no male children became destituted. These widows usually got the church to support them or some pious men. If the church supported the widow she would devote time to work: lighting candles, cleaning sacred vessels, and other tasks.

Thoughts

In this chapter the author has made the determination about the behavior, morals and ethics of the community.

Language

Peshitta	New American Standard 1995
1Tim. 6:1 Let them who are under the yoke of servitude, hold their masters in all honor; lest the name of God and his doctrine be reproached. ² And let them who have believing masters, not treat them with disrespect, because they are their brethren; but let them be more obedient, because they are believers and beloved, in whose service they enjoy quietness. These things teach thou, and request of them. ³ But if there be any one, who teacheth a different doctrine, and doth not accede to the salutary words of our Lord Jesus the Messiah, and to the doctrine of the fear of God, ⁴ he is one that exalteth himself, while he knoweth nothing; and he languisheth in the search and inquiry about words, from which come envy, and contention, and railing, and evil surmising, ⁵ and the disputation of men, whose minds are corrupt and destitute of the truth, and who suppose that gain is godliness. But from these stand thou aloof. ⁶ But great is our gain, which is the fear of God, with the use of our competence. ⁷ For we brought nothing into the world; and we know that we can carry nothing out of it. ⁸ Therefore, food and clothing satisfy us. ⁹ But they who desire to become rich, fall into temptations, and into snares, and into many lusts which are foolish and hurtful, and which drown men in destruction and perdition: ¹⁰ for the love of money is the	**1Tim. 6:1** ᵃAll who are under the yoke as slaves are to regard their own masters as worthy of all honor so ᵇthat the name of God and *our* doctrine will not be ¹spoken against. ² Those who have believers as their masters must not be disrespectful to them because they are ᵃbrethren, but must serve them all the more, because those who ¹partake of the benefit are believers and beloved. ᵇTeach and ²preach these *principles.* **1Tim. 6:3** If anyone ᵃadvocates a different doctrine and does not ¹agree with ᵇsound words, those of our Lord Jesus Christ, and with the doctrine ᶜconforming to godliness, ⁴ he is ᵃconceited *and* understands nothing; but he ¹has a morbid interest in ᵇcontroversial questions and ᶜdisputes about words, out of which arise envy, strife, abusive language, evil suspicions, ⁵ and constant friction between ᵃmen of depraved mind and deprived of the truth, who ᵇsuppose that ¹godliness is a means of gain. ⁶ ᵃBut godliness *actually* is a means of ᵇgreat gain when accompanied by ᶜcontentment. ⁷ For ᵃwe have brought nothing into the world, so we cannot take anything out of it either. ⁸ If we ᵃhave food and covering, with these we shall be content. ⁹ ᵃBut those who want to get rich fall into temptation and ᵇa snare and many foolish and harmful desires which plunge men into ruin and destruction. ¹⁰ For ᵃthe

root of all these evils. And there are some who, coveting it, have erred from the faith, and brought themselves into many sorrows. **11** But thou, O man of God, flee from these things; and follow after righteousness, and rectitude, and faith, and love, and patience, and humility. **12** And contend in the good contest of faith; and lay hold of life eternal, to which thou art called, and [of which] thou hast confessed a good confession before many witnesses. **13** I charge thee, before God, who quickeneth all, and [before] Jesus the Messiah who attested a good testimony before Pontius Pilate, **14** that thou keep the injunction, without stain, and without blemish, until the manifestation of our Lord Jesus the Messiah; **15** which God will, in due time make visible; [God] the blessed and only Potentate, the King of kings, and the Lord of lords; **16** who only is incorruptible, and dwelleth in light to which no one can approach; and whom no man hath seen, or even can see: to him be glory and dominion for ever and ever. Amen. **17** Charge the rich of this world, that they be not uplifted in their minds; and that they confide not in riches, in which is no security; but in the living God, who giveth us all things abundantly for our comfort: **18** and that they do good works, and be rich in well-doings; and be ready to give and to communicate: **19** and that they lay up for themselves a good foundation for that which is future; that they may take hold of real life. **20** O Timothy, be careful of that which is committed to thee; and shun vain words, and the oppositions of false science: **21** for they who profess it, have erred from the faith. Grace be with thee. Amen.

love of money is a root of all [1]sorts of evil, and some by longing for it have [b]wandered away from the faith and pierced themselves with many griefs.

1Tim. 6:11 But [a]flee from these things, you [b]man of God, and pursue righteousness, godliness, [c]faith, [d]love, [1]perseverance *and* gentleness. **12** [a]Fight the good fight of [b]faith; [c]take hold of the eternal life [d]to which you were called, and you made the good [e]confession in the presence of [f]many witnesses. **13** [a]I charge you in the presence of God, who [1]gives life to all things, and of [b]Christ Jesus, who testified the [c]good confession [d]before Pontius Pilate, **14** that you keep the commandment without stain or reproach until the [a]appearing of our Lord Jesus Christ, **15** which He will [1]bring about at [a]the proper time — He who is [b]the blessed and [c]only Sovereign, [d]the King of [2]kings and [e]Lord of [3]lords, **16** [a]who alone possesses immortality and [b]dwells in unapproachable light, [c]whom no man has seen or can see. [d]To Him *be* honor and eternal dominion! Amen.

1Tim. 6:17 Instruct those who are rich in [a]this present world [b]not to be conceited or to [c]fix their hope on the uncertainty of riches, but on God, [d]who richly supplies us with all things to enjoy. **18** *Instruct them* to do good, to be rich in [a]good [1]works, [b]to be generous and ready to share, **19** [a]storing up for themselves the treasure of a good foundation for the future, so that they may [b]take hold of that which is life indeed.

1Tim. 6:20 O [a]Timothy, guard [b]what has been entrusted to you, avoiding [c]worldly

<table>
<tr><td></td><td>

and empty chatter *and* the opposing arguments of what is falsely called "knowledge" — [21] which some have professed and thus [a]gone astray [1]from [b]the faith.

[c]Grace be with you.

</td></tr>
</table>

1Timothy 6:1
[1]Or *blasphemed*
[a]Eph 6:5; Titus 2:9; 1 Pet 2:18
[b]Titus 2:5

1Timothy 6:2
[1]Or *devote themselves to kindness*
[2]Lit *exhort, urge*
[a]Acts 1:15; Gal 3:28; Philem 16
[b]1 Tim 4:11

1Timothy 6:3
[1]Lit *come to;* or *come with*
[a]1 Tim 1:3
[b]1 Tim 1:10
[c]Titus 1:1

1Timothy 6:4
[1]Lit *is sick about*
[a]1 Tim 3:6
[b]1 Tim 1:4
[c]Acts 18:15; 2 Tim 2:14

1Timothy 6:5
[1]Or *religion*
[a]2 Tim 3:8; Titus 1:15
[b]Titus 1:11; 2 Pet 2:3

1Timothy 6:6
[a]Luke 12:15-21; 1 Tim 6:6-10
[b]1 Tim 4:8
[c]Phil 4:11; Heb 13:5

1Timothy 6:7
[a]Job 1:21; Eccl 5:15

1Timothy 6:8
[a]Prov 30:8

1Timothy 6:9
*a*Prov 15:27; 23:4; 28:20; Luke 12:21; 1 Tim 6:17
*b*1 Tim 3:7

1Timothy 6:10
[1]Lit *the evils*
*a*Col 3:5; 1 Tim 3:3; 6:9
*b*James 5:19

1Timothy 6:11
[1]Or *steadfastness*
*a*2 Tim 2:22
*b*2 Tim 3:17
*c*1 Tim 1:14
*d*2 Tim 3:10

1Timothy 6:12
*a*1 Cor 9:25f; Phil 1:30; 1 Tim 1:18
*b*1 Tim 1:19
*c*Phil 3:12; 1 Tim 6:19
*d*Col 3:15
*e*2 Cor 9:13; 1 Tim 6:13
*f*1 Tim 4:14; 2 Tim 2:2

1Timothy 6:13
[1]Or *preserves alive*
*a*1 Tim 5:21
*b*Gal 3:26; 1 Tim 1:12, 15; 2:5
*c*2 Cor 9:13; 1 Tim 6:12
*d*Matt 27:2; John 18:37

1Timothy 6:14
*a*2 Thess 2:8

1Timothy 6:15
[1]Lit *show*
[2]Lit *those who reign as kings*
[3]Lit *those who rule as lords*
*a*1 Tim 2:6
*b*1 Tim 1:11

[c]1 Tim 1:17
[d]Deut 10:17; Rev 17:14; 19:16
[e]Ps 136:3

1Timothy 6:16
[a]1 Tim 1:17
[b]Ps 104:2; James 1:17; 1 John 1:5
[c]John 1:18

1Timothy 6:17
[a]Matt 12:32; 2 Tim 4:10; Titus 2:12
[b]Ps 62:10; Luke 12:20; Rom 11:20; 1 Tim 6:9
[c]1 Tim 4:10
[d]Acts 14:17

1Timothy 6:18
[1]Or *deeds*
[a]1 Tim 5:10
[b]Rom 12:8; Eph 4:28

1Timothy 6:19
[a]Matt 6:20
[b]1 Tim 6:12

1Timothy 6:20
[a]1 Tim 1:2
[b]2 Tim 1:12, 14
[c]1 Tim 1:9; 2 Tim 2:16

1Timothy 6:21
[1]Lit *concerning*
[a]2 Tim 2:18
[b]1 Tim 1:19
[c]Col 4:18

Koine Greek

Language

Process of Discovery

Linguistics Section

Linguistic Structure

[Paul supports slavery] 1Tim. 6:1 *a*All who are under the yoke as slaves are to regard their own masters as worthy of all honor so *b*that the name of God and *our* doctrine will not be *1*spoken against. **2** Those who have believers as their masters must not be disrespectful to them because they are *a*brethren, but must serve them all the more, because those who *1*partake of the benefit are believers and beloved. *b*Teach and *2*preach these *principles.*

[Must follow Paul's ways] 1Tim. 6:3 If anyone *a*advocates a different doctrine and does not *1*agree with *b*sound words, those of our Lord Jesus Christ, and with the doctrine *c*conforming to godliness, **4** he is *a*conceited *and* understands nothing; but he *1*has a morbid interest in *b*controversial questions and *c*disputes about words, out of which arise envy, strife, abusive language, evil suspicions, **5** and constant friction between *a*men of depraved mind and deprived of the truth, who *b*suppose that *1*godliness is a means of gain. **6** *a*But godliness *actually* is a means of *b*great gain when accompanied by *c*contentment. **7** For *a*we have brought nothing into the world, so we cannot take anything out of it either. **8** If we *a*have food and covering, with these we shall be content. **9** *a*But those who want to get rich fall into temptation and *b*a snare and many foolish and harmful desires which plunge men into ruin and destruction. **10** For *a*the love of money is a root of all *1*sorts of evil, and some by longing for it have *b*wandered away from the faith and pierced themselves with many griefs.

[Must follow because Yeshua died] 1Tim. 6:11 But *a*flee from these things, you *b*man of God, and pursue righteousness, godliness, *c*faith, *d*love, *1*perseverance *and* gentleness. **12** *a*Fight the good fight of *b*faith; *c*take hold of the eternal life *d*to which you were called, and you made the good *e*confession in the presence of *f*many witnesses. **13** *a*I charge you in the presence of God, who *1*gives life to all things, and of *b*Christ Jesus, who testified the *c*good confession *d*before Pontius Pilate, **14** that you keep the commandment without stain or reproach until the *a*appearing of our Lord Jesus Christ, **15** which He will *1*bring about at *a*the proper time — He who is *b*the blessed and *c*only Sovereign, *d*the King of *2*kings and *e*Lord of *3*lords, **16** *a*who alone possesses immortality and *b*dwells in unapproachable light, *c*whom no man has seen or can see. *d*To Him *be* honor and eternal dominion! Amen.

[Teach the rich] 1Tim. 6:17 Instruct those who are rich in *a*this present world *b*not to be conceited or to *c*fix their hope on the uncertainty of riches, but on God, *d*who richly supplies us with all things to enjoy. **18** *Instruct them* to do good, to be rich in *ᵃ*good ¹works, *ᵇ*to be generous and ready to share, **19** *ᵃ*storing up for themselves the treasure of a good foundation for the future, so that they may *ᵇ*take hold of that which is life indeed.

[Ending comments] 1Tim. 6:20 O *ᵃ*Timothy, guard *ᵇ*what has been entrusted to you, avoiding *ᶜ*worldly *and* empty chatter *and* the opposing arguments of what is falsely called "knowledge" — **21** which some have professed and thus *ᵃ*gone astray ¹from *ᵇ*the faith. *ᶜ*Grace be with you.

Discussion

Questioning the Passage

 Verse Comparison of citations or proof text

Translation Inconsistencies

Biblical Personalities

Biblical Locations

Phrase Study

Linguistic Echoes

Rules of Hillel

Culture Section

Discussion